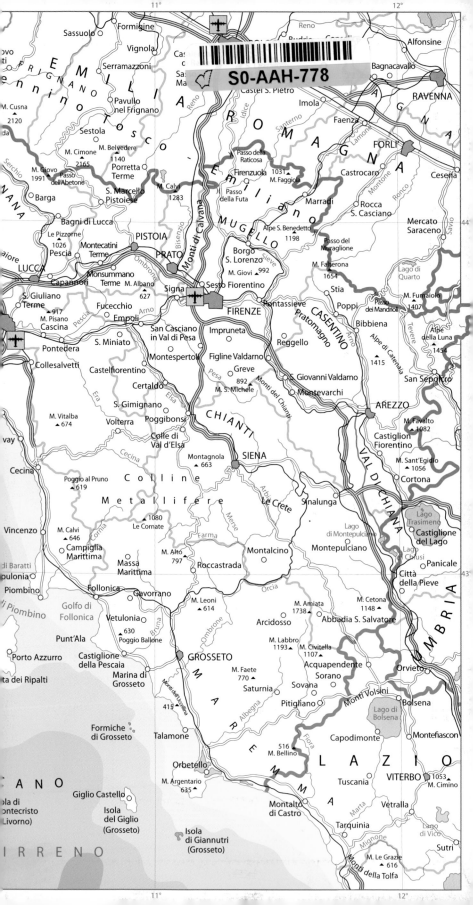

FLORENCE
AND
TUSCANY

A COMPLETE GUIDE WITH ITINERARIES

**ats
italia
editrice**

Table of contents

HISTORICAL NOTES

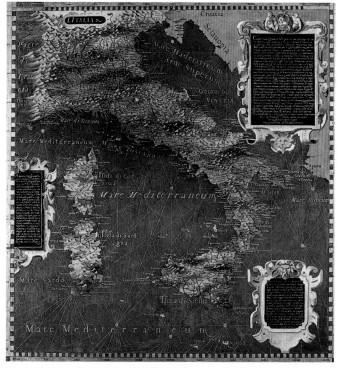

Florence, Palazzo Vecchio, Hall of the Maps, ancient map of Italy

Set in the North-centre of Italy, Tuscany has been the heart of Italy's artistic and historical events throughout several centuries. The largest and most civilised free communes and city-states mushroomed in this region, that was also the cradle of Renaissance and of a Tuscan-derived language that was to become the national language, the language of Dante Alighieri, a poet from Florence. Tuscany eventually derived its name from Tusci, another name for the Etruscans, whose civilisation sprung in this region. Taken over by Rome at the end of the IV Century B.C., ancient Etruria, which extended to reach the river Tiber, had already become a province of the diocese of Italy, with the name of Tuscia, by the second half of that same century. It was a Lombard Duchy in the VI century. In 774 the Carolingians conquered Tuscany and established their control over the region, supported by the Counts of Lucca, who adopted the title of Marquises of Tuscany in the century that followed. This dynasty saw its downfall in 1115, with the death of Countess Matilda, who had been a distinguished and skilled diplomat and had successfully encouraged Pope Gregory VII and Emperor Henry IV to meet in her Castle in Canossa. In her will, Matilda had bequeathed her rich possession to the Church.

However, the German Emperors refused to acknowledge the Countess' testamentary dispositions, which further intensified the controversies between Church and Empire. Therefore, some Tuscan cities, rallying in opposition to both the rival parties, declared their independence and enacted their own laws. Such were the first Tuscan Communes, followed by Seignories and later by actual States (Florence, Siena, Pisa, Lucca etc.), cradles of Tuscan history up to 1530, when the Medici family re-established their power. In 1569, Cosimo I Medici had obtained the title of Grand Duke of Tuscany by Pope Pius V, he therefore consolidated the power of Florence throughout the region. Massa and Carrara, Piombino and the Republic of Lucca remained independent from the Medici Princedom, though they only enjoyed limited autonomy in the absence of significant outlets. With Cosimo II (1609-1621) and Ferdinand II (1621-1670) the economy had been slowly but consistently stagnating, followed by a severe decline in its grasp on the international scene. The economy further declined under the rule of Cosimo III (1670-1723) and Gian Gastone (1723-1737). The European powers, while foreseeing the dynasty's extinction, arranged that regency would pass to Charles I, son of Philip V of Spain, followed by Francesco Stefano of Lorraine (1737-1765), husband of the future Queen Maria Teresa. Annexed to the Napoleonic Empire in 1807, Tuscany was once again turned into a Grand Duchy for Elisa Bonaparte Baciocchi, who, however, had to relinquish it to Ferdinand III on September 1814. Once again under the rule of the House of Hapsburg (Ferdinand III, 1814-24; Leopold II 1824-59; Ferdinand IV, 1859-60), Tuscany was incorporated into the Dukedom of Lucca. The region, which suffered the paternalistic despotism of its rulers, rose up against them in 1848 and, by February 1849, it became a republic under a triumvirate, whose members were Mazzoni, Guerrazzi and Montanelli. Nevertheless, the Austrian troops secured Grand Duke Leopold II's return to power (July 1849). In 1859, at the outbreak of the new war between Piedmont and Austria, revolutionary agitation sprang up once again and the Grand Duke was forced to go back to Vienna (which happened in April 27, 1859). A temporary government, under the direction of Peruzzi, followed by Ricasoli (who was also to become the head of the Italian Government following Cavour's death in 1861), declared war against Austria. Napoleon III was about to carry out his plans and create a State in Central Italy, that he would have granted to Giordano Napoleone, when Tuscans prevented him from making his move by choosing to merge with the Reign of Sardinia (March 1860). After the Unification of Italy, Tuscany followed the fortunes of the other regions, though with a remarkable difference: in anticipation of the conquest of Rome, Florence replaced Turin (despite the latter's wildfire of political discontent) and became the capital of the Unified Italy (1865-1871). The weight of burdens, however, exceeded by far that of glory for two main reasons. First, the invasion of bureaucrats from the Government of the House of Savoy caused a steep rise in the cost of living. Second, to propel it to the same status as Turin, the city underwent vast transformations.

As a result, the city's Medieval centre was destroyed, along with the Old Market and the city walls. For six years Florence had no benefits from all this; instead, it had to bear the high costs of court life. Tuscan history from that point onwards was intertwined with that of the rest of Italy. Despite this, the region kept its own artistic and literary tradition. Besides being the country of adoption of famous Italian and foreign artists and writers, in the years between the two World Wars Tuscany and its capital became the cradle and backdrop of the activity of writers and painters, many of whom were born Tuscan. Almost all of them stood out as the most important artists of XX-century Italy.

Florence, Cappella dei Principi, Medicean coat of arms on the floor

itinerary

1

FLORENCE
- THE BAPTISTERY
- CATHEDRAL OF SANTA MARIA DEL FIORE
- MUSEUM OF THE OPERA DEL DUOMO
- LOGGIA DEL BIGALLO
- CHURCH OF ORSANMICHELE
- PALAZZO DELL'ARTE DELLA LANA
- PIAZZA DELLA SIGNORIA
- PALAZZO VECCHIO
- LOGGIA DELLA SIGNORIA
- LOGGIA DEL MERCATO NUOVO
- UFFIZI GALLERY
- PONTE VECCHIO
- PALAZZO PITTI
- BOBOLI GARDENS
- CHURCH OF SANTO SPIRITO
- CHURCH OF SANTA MARIA DEL CARMINE
- BASILICA OF SAN LORENZO
- LAURENTIAN MEDICI LIBRARY
- MEDICEAN CHAPELS
- MEDICI RICCARDI PALACE
- CHURCH AND MONASTERY OF SAN MARCO
- GALLERIA DELL'ACCADEMIA
- OPIFICIO DELLE PIETRE DURE
- BASILICA OF SANTA CROCE
- PALAZZO DEL BARGELLO
- BADIA FIORENTINA
- DANTE'S HOUSE
- CIVIC MUSEUM "FIRENZE COM'ERA"
- CHURCH OF SS. ANNUNZIATA
- ARCHAEOLOGICAL MUSEUM
- PIAZZA DELLA REPUBBLICA
- PALAZZO DAVANZATI
- CHURCH OF SANTA TRINITA
- PALAZZO STROZZI
- PALAZZO RUCELLAI
- CHURCH OF SANTA MARIA NOVELLA
- PIAZZALE MICHELANGELO
- CHURCH OF SAN MINIATO AL MONTE
- CHARTERHOUSE AT GALLUZZO

ITS SURROUNDINGS:
- FIESOLE
- SAN DOMENICO
- BADIA FIESOLANA
- CERTALDO
- CHIANTI
- EMPOLI
- MONTESENARIO
- MUGELLO
- VALLOMBROSA
- VINCI

FLORENCE AND ITS SURROUNDINGS

o del
glione
erona
4
tia
Poppi Passo
dei Mandrioli
Bibbiena
TINO
aldarno San Sepolcro
chi
AREZZO
Castiglion
Fiorentino
Cortona
a
Lago
Montepulciano
epulciano
M. Cetona
1148
badia S. Salvatore
ndente
o

FLORENCE

Florence was founded approximately in the X century B.C., in the Arno valley, at the junction of the two rivers: Mugnone and Arno. In 59 B.C., after the Roman Emperor Caesar had passed a land reform, the town was built to meet the criteria of a military camp ("castrum militare"); its ancient main roads can still be seen in the old city centre. This first settlement, surrounded by walls, was named Florentia and it prospered indeed, so that it became the seat of the Governor of Tuscany and Umbria (278-366 A.D.). Following the timeline of events over the centuries, the city managed to halt the barbarian invasions, but could not avoid being drawn into the orbit of the Byzantine Empire (541 A.D.). As a result, the city had to reduce the wall perimeter to a more modest size, since its walls had become far too large for a city that had depopulated and could barely count a thousand inhabitants.

Approximately in the year 1000, Florence was the political centre of the March of Tuscany, governed by Marquis Ugo. The city experienced enough of a revival in terms of its economic development, requiring the city walls, referred to by Dante as the "cerchia antica" (the old ring), to be extended in 1078.

At the end of the XII century, Florence was an autonomous Commune under the rule of a powerful bourgeoisie organised in corporate associations of artisans and merchants; commerce was dramatically intensified, which led to a demographic expansion – the city had a population of 30,000 – and new walls were built between 1173 and 1175. Tower-houses were erected that, if necessary, could serve as defensive fortresses connected to each other, in which members of the two opposing factions could seek refuge: the Guelphs, supporters of the Pope, and the Ghibellins, supporters of the Emperor. After a series of adverse events, the Guelphs managed to finally defeat their adversaries and Florence became a seigneury under the rule of Priors, elected among the members of the Guilds (ancient Corporations divided in Major and Minor Crafts).

One outstanding piece of evidence of Florence's economic expansion was the launch of the gold florin, minted by the city Government, which became an exceptionally sound currency at the time. Many Florentine families became money-lenders and changers, paving the way for progenies of rich bankers such as the Medici family, the fortunes of which are entangled inextricably with the history of Florence. Between 1284 and 1333, large new city walls were erected and the city underwent intensive urban development, envisaging both public and private interventions. In 1347 a vast epidemic of black death killed more than 50% of the population and the city economy suffered a dramatic setback, when almost all construction sites and workshops closed. Florence rose to economic and cultural pre-eminence in the XV century, with a period of economic growth and prosperity, largely due to the Medici family's intelligence: it was especially under Cosimo the Old (1389-64) and Lorenzo the Magnificent (1449-92) that Florence became most prestigious. This is how the leading role of the Medici dynasty began, with Florence remaining under their rule until the XVIII century. They were first granted the honorary title of Lords of the city (thus becoming the most important family in town), then that of Dukes, to eventually be elevated to the status of Grand Dukes of Tuscany. When the family died out, the Grand Duchy passed into the hands of the House of Lorraine, who ruled until 1860, when Florence and Tuscany completely merged with the new Kingdom of Italy, with the city of the flower as its capital from 1865 to 1871. In the XX century, when turned into one of the major tourist destinations, offering a chance to live amidst the greatest masterpieces in the history of art, Florence suffered two historically relevant events: the bombings of World War II (1940-44) and the devastating flood of November 4, 1966.Despite these two catastrophes, the city regained its splendour along with its artistic and moral traditions and became a real world heritage.

THE BAPTISTERY Dedicated to San Giovanni Battista, Saint protector of the city, it features an octagonal structure in a clean Florentine-Romanesque style, and is covered with Carrara-white and Prato-green marble. Its dome features an eight-segment structure, externally masked by the perimeter walls and covered by a flattened pyramid roof. Today's baptistery was built between the XI and the XIII centuries, on a pre-existing Roman building, dating back to the IV-V centuries.

It has three famous entrance doors: the South Door by Andrea Pisano (1330-1338), with its twenty top quatrefoil panels featuring episodes from the life of St John the Baptist, and the eight lower ones depicting the Christian Virtues; the North Door by Lorenzo Ghiberti (1403-1424), featuring twenty top panels, plus eight lower panels depicting the Evangelists and the four Church Fathers; the

on the left:
Andrea Pisano,
South Door
on the right:
Lorenzo Ghiberti,
North Door

East Door, known as the *Gates of Paradise*, also by Lorenzo Ghi-berti (1425-1452), depicts scenes from the Old Testament. The beautiful internal pavement features a complex marble mosaic. Its dome ceiling is covered with magnificent XII-century mosaics and is dominated by Jesus Christ as Judge.

The horizontal tiers of the mosaics feature stories of St John the Baptist, of Jesus Christ, St Joseph and the book of Genesis. The top centre of the dome is decorated with mosaics depicting the Choirs of Angels.

on the left:
Lorenzo Ghiberti, East Door,
known as the *Gates of Paradise*
below:
Panel with scenes from the life
of Joseph, original panel of the
Gates of Paradise
Museum of the Opera del Duomo
below:
Baptistery, mosaics,
interior of the Dome

CATHEDRAL OF SANTA MARIA DEL FIORE Its construction began in September 1296 to the design of Arnolfo di Cambio, with the Republic bearing the costs of its erection, along with the Guild of the Wool Merchants, supervising works until its designer died in 1301.

It was dedicated to the Virgin Mary: the Flower stands for both Christ and the city. Giotto was the master builder from 1334 to 1337, followed by Andrea Pisano and Francesco Talenti. Filippo Brunelleschi was commissioned to design its dome (1418-1436) and Pope Eugene IV consecrated it in 1436. Its building and completion took all of 140 years.

The cathedral features an octagonal structure with a total height of 106 metres and exterior walls entirely lined with polychrome marble featuring geometrical patterns. Its neo-gothic facade was built and completed between 1871 and 1887 by Emilio de Fabris. The whole design forms a Latin cross with three naves, built in a pure Florentine-Gothic style. A colossal clock can be seen on its counter-facade, decorated by Paolo Uccello in 1443.

The third span of the left nave features two frescoes: the *Equestrian Monument of Giovanni Acuto* by Paolo Uccello (1436) and

Paolo Uccello,
Clock indicating
the *canonical hours*

Cathedral, interior

the *Equestrian Monument of Niccolò da Tolentino* by Andrea del Castagno (1456). The fourth span of that same nave features a painting by Domenico di Michelino, depicting *Dante and his Divine Comedy* (1465). The Dome interior is frescoed with scenes from the *Last Judgement* by Vasari (1572-74) and by Federico Zuccari (1578-79).

The BELL TOWER, with its 85-metre height is among the most outstanding examples of Florence XIII-century Gothic architecture. It was begun in 1334 to the design of Giotto, who worked at it until 1337, when he died. His successors were Andrea Pisano, Alberto Arnoldi, Maso di Bacco and Luca della Robbia. The original panels decorating the bell tower are now housed in the Museum of the Opera del Duomo.

Giorgio Vasari and Federico Zuccari, Cathedral, frescoes of the dome interior

Michelangelo, Pietà

on the right:
Donatello, Choir loft

MUSEUM OF THE OPERA DEL DUOMO The Opera del Duomo was founded in 1296, in order to build the Cathedral of Santa Maria del Fiore and administrate the funds provided for the purpose. The museum, however, was only established in 1891. It houses important artworks removed from the Cathedral, the Bell Tower and the Baptistery, among which are Michelangelo's *Pietà* (roughly 1550-53), Donatello's *Choir loft* and *Maddalena* (1433-39) and Luca della Robbia's *Choir loft* (1431-38).

LOGGIA DEL BIGALLO It is a brilliant example of civil and religious architecture merged into a single building; designed by Arnoldi, it was built from 1352 to 1358 for the Confraternity of Mercy.

Loggia del Bigallo

ORSANMICHELE First known as the Church of San Michele in Orto, the building was originally a loggia built around 1337 for the grain market, to the design of Francesco Talenti, Neri di Fioravante and Benci di Cione. In 1380 it was transformed into a church and externally decorated with the statues of the Guilds' *Patron Saints*, carved between the XV and the XVII centuries (noteworthy is Donatello's *Tabernacle with St George*, dating back to 1416). Its interior houses the superb *Tabernacle* by Andrea Orcagna (1349-59) depicting the *theological Virtues and scenes from the Virgin's life.*

Orsanmichele is connected via a flyover, built in 1569 and transformed at the beginning of the XX century, to the

below:
Flyover connecting the
Palazzo dell'Arte della Lana
to Orsanmichele's
on the right:
Church of Orsanmichele

PALAZZO DELL'ARTE DELLA LANA The building was the seat of one of the most powerful and richest Guilds; built in 1308, it was restored in 1905.

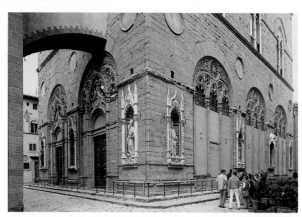

PIAZZA DELLA SIGNORIA This is undoubtedly one of the most beautiful squares worldwide. Excavations brought Roman archaeological finds to light, along with traces of more ancient civilisations, which provided evidence of the area being inhabited back in the Bronze Age. In the XIII and XIV centuries it became the cradle of Florence city-life.

A painting of the time depicting
Girolamo Savonarola
burnt at the stake (1498).
Noteworthy is the original floor
of the square in cotto tiles,
with Tuscan sandstone stripes
organised in a grid pattern.
This painting is displayed
at the Museum of San Marco.

The square is an authentic open-air museum. Starting from the left there is the *Equestrian Monument of Cosimo I de'Medici* (1594) by Giambologna, the *Fonte di Piazza,* also known as the *Fountain of Neptune* (1563-75), by Bartolomeo Ammannati and others, a copy of *Judith and Holophern* by Donatello (1455-60), a copy of the *David* by Michelangelo (1504), *Hercules and Cacus* by Bandinelli (1533).

A glimpse on the square: in plain sight are
Hercules and Cacus, followed by a copy of
Michelangelo's David and Bartolomeo
Ammannati's Neptune

Piazza della Signoria,
Equestrian Monument of Cosimo I

Michelozzo's courtyard,
decorated by Vasari.
In the middle, Andrea
Verrocchio, fountain
surmounted by the Winged
Cherub with Fish (a copy)

PALAZZO VECCHIO Also known as PALAZZO DELLA SIGNORIA. The main building was erected between 1299 and 1314 to the design of Arnolfo di Cambio, who also designed the superb 1310 tower, 94 metres tall, dominating the mighty structure of this Gothic Palace.

It accommodated Tuscany temporary Government (1848-49 and 1859-60) as well as the Chamber of Deputies of the United Italy, at the time Florence was its capital. Since 1872 it has been the seat of Florence local Government. Its interior is finely and sumptuously decorated from its very first courtyard, decorated by Vasari in 1565. In the middle of the courtyard stands the copy of Verrocchio's *Winged Cherub with Fish* (1476).

Its first floor accommodates the magnificent *"Hall of the Five Hundred"* by Simone del Pollaiolo (known as *il Cronaca*), dated 1495; its coffered ceiling features 39 wood panel paintings by Vasari (1563-1565) with the *Allegories and Scenes from the History of Florence and the Medici Family*.

Its Western wall houses the *Private Study of Francesco I,* by both Vasari and Bronzino (1570-72). The second floor houses the *Apartments of Eleonora*, the *Apartments of the Elements*, the *Hall of the Lilies,* and the *Wardrobe*. Several restoration works have been carried out recently, both for the facade and the Bell Tower.

Restorations carried out inside the Palace have made it possible to equip the building with multimedia facilities to take tourists on interesting virtual tours.

Hall of the Five Hundred

Loggia della Signoria

next page:
Loggia della Signoria,
Benvenuto Cellini, Perseus

Loggia della Signoria,
Giambologna,
Rape of the Sabine Women

LOGGIA DELLA SIGNORIA also known as loggia DELL'ORCAGNA. It was named after the nickname of Andrea di Cione, who possibly designed it; Benci di Cione and Simone di Francesco Talenti supervised its construction between 1376 and 1382, when it was completed. Among others, the building houses the statues of *Perseus* by Benvenuto Cellini (1545-54) and the *Rape of the Sabine Women* by Giambologna (1583).

From Piazza della Signoria take Via Vacchereccia, to reach the

LOGGIA DEL MERCATO NUOVO It is also known as *mercato del porcellino* (market of the piglet) for the presence of a bronze statue by Pietro Tacca (circa 1612), featuring a wild boar; the market was built by G. Battista del Tasso (1547 to 1551).

Loggia del Mercato Nuovo known as *Market of the Piglet*

room 2:
Cimabue,
Majesty

room 6:
Gentile da Fabriano,
Adoration of the Magi

room 7:
Piero della Francesca,
Portrait of Federico da Montefeltro

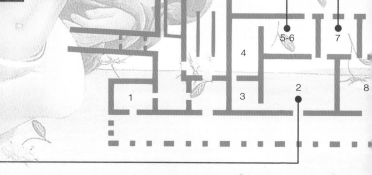

room 44:
Rembrandt,
Self-portrait

room 43:
Caravaggio,
Medusa

room 33:
Bronzino,
Deposition

room 10-14:
Botticelli,
Madonna of the Magnificat

room 20:
Lukas Cranack the Old,
Eve

room 26:
Andrea del Sarto,
Madonna of the Harpies

16

10-14   15   17   18   19   20   21   22   23   24

41   36-37   35   34   25

38   26

33   27

32   28

31   29   30

room 31:
Dosso Dossi,
Witchcraft

room 29:
Parmigianino,
Madonna of the Long Neck

room 28:
Tiziano,
Venus of Urbino

Uffizi Gallery, exterior

UFFIZI GALLERY The building was erected for Cosimo I, in order to bring the administrative offices of the Tuscan State under the same roof. Designed by Vasari, it was built between 1560 and 1580 and completed by Alfonso Parigi and Bernardo Buontalenti. It is one of the most important museums worldwide, housing a selection of outstanding masterpieces, located on the second floor of this same building. Here is a display of paintings of the Florentine tradition, for a period spanning from the XIV to the XVI century. Among these are Cimabue, Duccio and Giotto's masterpieces (*Madonna d'Ognissanti* or All Saints Altaripiece, approximately 1310), along with Simone Martini, Paolo Uccello, Piero della Francesca, Masaccio, Botticelli (*Birth of Venus*, 1486; the *Primavera*, 1477-78), Leonardo da Vinci and Michelangelo's (*Doni Rounded* 1504-05). Just as outstanding are the halls dedicated to the Italian and to the European painters, among which are Raffaello (*Madonna of the Goldfinch,* 1506), Tiziano, Caravaggio, along with Rembrandt and the XII-century Flemish painters. Also worth seeing is the *Tribune*, designed by Buontalenti (1585-89), to house the first Medici collection. On leaving the museum, past Por Santa Maria, you will find Ponte Vecchio.

Giotto, Majesty

on the right:
Michelangelo,
Doni Roundel

Botticelli, the Birth of Venus

Leonardo da Vinci, Annunciation

Filippo Lippi, Madonna with Child and Angels

Raffaello, Madonna of the Goldfinch

Caravaggio, adolescent Bacchus

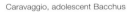

Tribune

PONTE VECCHIO It was already there at the time of the Romans and is the most ancient bridge in Florence; its present structure dates back to 1345, when Neri Floravanti built it. Already at that time it housed shops that sold food, which were replaced with jewelleries and goldsmiths in 1500. On its East-side runs the Vasari Corridor, built for Cosimo I de' Medici, to the design of Vasari (1565).

It allowed the Grand Duke to go from his residence (Palazzo Pitti) to the Government Palace (Palazzo Vecchio) undisturbed. The corridor still connects Palazzo Pitti to the Uffizi Gallery. Past the Old Bridge on the River Arno, via Guicciardini leads to Piazza Pitti, dominated by the Palace bearing the same name.

Palazzo Pitti, rear

PALAZZO PITTI It is the largest XV-century palace in Florence. It was built in *rustic style* by Luca Fancelli in 1457, to the design of Filippo Brunelleschi (circa 1440), for the banker Luca Pitti. It was enlarged by Bartolomeo Ammannati when the Medici family bought it and made it their residence (XVI century). Further extensions were carried out in the following century. Palazzo Pitti today houses valuable treasures: the Galleria Palatina displays Italian and Foreign artworks, almost entirely from the Medici's private collection. Among these is a wonderful collection made up of 11 paintings by Raffaello (among which are the *Madonna of the Chair* and the *Madonna of the Grand Duke*), along with works by Tiziano, Tintoretto, Rubens and Van Dyck. The Royal Apartments, formerly used by the Medicis and then lived in by their successors of the House of Lorraine and by the Savoys for a short time, still house the original, lavish furniture. The Silverware Museum displays objects from the Grand Dukes' Treasure: jewels, ivory and crystal ware, furniture, china and glass ware. The Gallery of Modern Art houses paintings and sculptures from the XIX and the XX century and its main collection includes paintings by artists of the Macchiaioli movement, among which are Lega, Fattori and Signorini. Last but not least, the fancy Costume Gallery displays dresses and accessories for a time span ranging from the end of the XVII century to the XX century. Annexed to this Palace are the amazing Boboli Gardens.

Boboli Gardens, one of its internal alleys

BOBOLI GARDENS Eleonore of Toledo, wife of Cosimo I, bought the gardens from the Pitti family in 1550. Niccolò Pericoli, known as *Tribolo*, started to organise them, at least at a first stage. After his death, Davide Fortini and Giorgio Vasari took his place. Niccolò Ammanati designed the courtyard still bearing his name. The architecture of the beautiful artificial grotto, the *Grotta Grande*, with lateral niches housing the statues of *Bacchus* and *Cerere*, outstanding works by Baccio Bandinelli, is by Bernardo Buontalenti.

Out of Palazzo Pitti, turn into the sdrucciolo de' Pitti, then into Via Maggio, to reach Piazza Santo Spirito.

CHURCH OF SANTO SPIRITO

Started by Brunelleschi in 1444, it was extended with a vestibule and a sacristy, built at the end of the XV century by Cronaca and Giuliano da Sangallo. Its interior houses a *wooden Crucifix* by Michelangelo Buonarroti.

Church of Santo Spirito

Church of Santo Spirito, interior

Michelangelo, wooden Crucifix

From Piazza Santo Spirito, turn right into Via San Agostino, to reach the

CHURCH OF SANTA MARIA DEL CARMINE

Built between the XIII and the XV century, it was rebuilt after the devastating fire of 1771. Luckily enough its sacristy, the Corsini Chapel and the famous Brancacci Chapel, with frescoes by Masolino da Panicale and by Masaccio (1424-25), survived the fire. When Masaccio died, Filippino Lippi (1481) completed the works. The Brancacci chapel is home to frescoes that are considered to be early-Renaissance masterpiece.

Brancacci Chapel,
Masolino da Panicale and Masaccio,
Expulsion from the Garden of Eden

The Brancacci Chapel, right wall, Masolino da Panicale and Masaccio,
Healing of the cripple and resurrection of Tabitha

Basilica of San Lorenzo,
Old Sacristy

BASILICA OF SAN LORENZO This basilica claims ancient origins. Nothing in the building seems to correspond to the original plan. The basilica was apparently consecrated in 393 by St Ambrose and dedicated to Lawrence the martyr. The current building, paid by the Medici family, who turned it into a family's church, was built to the design of Filippo Brunelleschi in 1420. It is one of the most outstanding examples of Renaissance architecture. Its undecorated facade was actually never completed: the original project forsaw a marble facing that was never made. Its interior opens up into the Old Sacristy (Brunelleschi, 1420-29), decorated with medallions and lunettes by Donatello (1435-43), also displaying the *Burial of Giovanni di Bicci* (1434) in the middle. The latter was the progenitor of the Medici family. On the left wall stands the *Tomb of Piero and Giovanni de'Medici* (1472) by Andrea del Verrocchio.

LAURENTIAN MEDICI LIBRARY The cloister of the Basilica leads to the Laurentian Medici Library. Designed by Michelangelo in 1524, it houses more than 10,000 manuscripts of the Medici family, something like 70,000 books, over 400 incunabula and over 4,000 XVI-century editions, along with one of the most valuable collections of Egyptian papyri worldwide.

Laurentian Medici Library,
below: the vestibule
on the right: the reading room

On leaving the Church of San Lorenzo, cross the square to reach Piazza Madonna degli Aldobrandini, where you can visit the

MEDICEAN CHAPELS These include the Cappella dei Principi (Princes' Chapel) and the Sacrestia Nuova (New Sacristy) and are the mausoleum of the Medici Family. The imposing, octagonal Chapel of the Princes features a baroque structure with valuable marble and hard-stone revetments. Built in 1604 to the design of Matteo Nigetti for Grand Duke Ferdinand I de'Medici, it was aimed at housing the tombs of the Grand Dukes of Tuscany. The New Sacristy was built to the design of Michelangelo, who also authored its sculptures (1521), but could not complete the building, as he had to leave Florence in 1534. Instead, it was completed by Vasari and by Ammanniti in 1555, and houses the tombs of Lorenzo, Count of Urbino, and Giuliano, Duke of Nemours, their statues standing with those of the allegories of *Day*, *Night*, *Dawn* and *Dusk*, most evocative and perfect in their shapes, so as to be considered by many critics the best sculptures of all times.

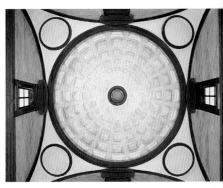

Medicean Chapels,
dome of the Cappella dei Principi

From Piazza San Lorenzo, through Via de' Gori, you can reach the

PALAZZO MEDICI RICCARDI Built to the design of Michelozzo (circa 1444-64) for Cosimo the Old, it was extended in the XVII-XVIII centuries, when it was bought by the Riccardi family. Today it is the seat of the Province of Florence, also hosting temporary exhibitions by the great interpreters of Renaissance and Baroque art. The *Chapel of the Magi* by Michelozzo is on the first floor, with frescoes by Benozzo Gozzoli (1459-60) such as the *Cavalcade of the Magi*, a narrative masterpiece, renowned for its ornamental and figurative richness.

Medicean Chapels,
vault of the New Sacristy

On leaving the Palace, walk through via Cavour, to reach Piazza San Marco, dominated by the ancient Monastery of San Marco.

on the left:
Palazzo Medici Riccardi

below:
Chapel of the Magi, right wall,
Benozzo Gozzoli,
a detail of the Cavalcade of the Magi

Church of San Marco

CHURCH AND MONASTERY OF SAN MARCO Today's building is the result of the restoration works carried out by Michelozzo (1437-52) for Cosimo the Old. This is the monastery where, besides Friar Gerolamo Savonarola, Beato Angelico lived, who also authored its splendid frescoes. Remarkable is the *Crucifixion* (1441-42) in the *Chapter Hall* and the famous *Annunciation* in front of the stairs leading to the first floor. Here are the friars' cells, also frescoed by Friar Angelico (1439-45), and the Library designed by Michelozzo.

on the right:
Monastery of San Marco, internal yard

Beato Angelico, Annunciation

From Piazza San Marco access Via Ricasoli, where you will find the

ACADEMY GALLERY Grand Duke Pietro Leopoldo founded it in 1784 to allow students from the nearby Academy of Fine Arts to exercise by taking the wonderful paintings of Florentine tradition as examples for their works. Besides housing many paintings by Florentine artists, dating back to the XIV and the XVI centuries, the gallery displays some of the most outstanding sculptures by Michelangelo, among which his *David*, deemed to be the great artist's most famous masterpiece. The colossal marble statue (with its 4,10-metre-tall standing-figure) is on display together with the four *Prisoners* and the *Pietà di Palestrina*.

Corridor or Room of the Academy

Michelangelo, Palestrina Pietà

Michelangelo, David

Botticelli, Madonna with Child, S. Giovannino and Angels

From Via Ricasoli, turn left into Via degli Alfani, to reach the

OPIFICIO DELLE PIETRE DURE This is a peculiar museum, displaying semi-precious stone-creations produced from the XVII to the XIX century, in the workshops of specialised artists and in the Institute founded in 1588, by Grand Duke Ferdinand I.

Middle nave

A detail of the floor scattered with tomb slabs

Stefano Ricci,
Cenotaph of Dante Alighieri

Innocenzo Spinazzi,
Tomb of Niccolo Machiavelli

BASILICA OF SANTA CROCE Construction of the church began in 1294, to the design of Arnolfo di Cambio. It was consecrated in 1443 and has always been the main seat of the Florentine Franciscan Friars, besides being considered the most beautiful Gothic church in Italy. Its neo-gothic facade, in rough stone and brick, is by Niccolò Matas (1853-63).

The triple-nave interior features headstones and Tombs of quite a few illustrious Florentines, made by great artists: the right nave houses *Michelangelo's Tomb* (Vasari, 1570); the *Cenotaph of Dante Alighieri* (Stefano Ricci, 1829), the *Monument of Vittorio Alfieri* (Canova, 1810), *Niccolò Machiavelli's Tomb* (Spinazzi, 1787), the *Monument of Leonardo Bruni* (Rossellino, approximately 1447), *Gioacchino Rossini's Tomb* (Cassioli, XIX century). Behind the fifth altar there is the magnificent sandstone relief of the *Annunciation* by Donatello (1435); the head-volume of the right-hand transept houses the *Bardi and the Peruzzi Chapels*, frescoed by Giotto after 1317; the left nave features *Galileo Galilei's Tomb* (Foggini, 1737).

Just nearby the church is the entrance to the Museum of the Opera of Santa Croce, with its *Pazzi Chapel*, designed by Brunelleschi in 1443 for Andrea Pazzi and decorated with terracottas by Luca della Robbia.

The Refectory displays the famous *Crucifix* by Cimabue (end of the XIII century), restored after the extensive damage suffered, due to the flood that hit Florence in 1966.

Cross Piazza Santa Croce, turn right into Via Verdi, then left into Via Ghibellina, to reach the

PALAZZO DEL BARGELLO The Palazzo del Podestà, which later became the headquarters of the Chief of Police (the Bargello or Captain of Justice), was built in 1255 as the seat of the Florentine Captaincy. Since 1859 the Palace has accommodated the National Museum bearing the same name, also housing sculptures and decorative works of art. A room in the ground-floor houses some famous sculptures by Michelangelo, among which are *Brutus* (1539), *Bacchus* (1497-99) and the *Pitti Roundel*, the *Bust of Cosimo I* (1546-57) by Benvenuto Cellini and works by Giambologna. The Hall of the General Council on the first floor displays the *David* (1430) and *St George* (1416) by Donatello; on the second floor are some famous terracottas by Della Robbias, as well as some Renaissance sculptures (works by Sansovino, Pollaiolo, Verrocchio).

Palazzo del Bargello

Luca della Robbia,
Madonna of the rose garden

Michelangelo,
Madonna with Child, *(Pitti Roundel)*

Donatello, David

Right opposite the Palazzo del Bargello there is the

BADIA FIORENTINA also known as the CHURCH OF SANTA MARIA ASSUNTA DELLA BADIA FIORENTINA. Named after the Benedictine abbey it is annexed to, it was built in 978 and entirely restored in 1285 by Arnolfo di Cambio, besides being reworked over the following centuries. On entering it, right on the left, there is the *Madonna appearing to St Bernard* by Filippino Lippi (approximately 1485) and, entering the left transept, also the *Tomb of Count Ugo* by Mino da Fiesole. Worth seeing is the *Chiostro degli Aranci*, a wonderful cloister by Bernardo Rossellino (1438), in an exquisite Florentine, early-Renaissance style.

Badia Fiorentina

On leaving the Abbey, walk down Via Dante Alighieri until you find

Dante's House

DANTE'S HOUSE It was arbitrarily restored in modern times (1875-1910) and nowadays accommodates a small museum dedicated to Dante's works; this is where the Alighieri's towers were erected.

Walking back along the Via Dante Alighieri, you will find Via del Proconsolo, leading to Piazza del Duomo; Once there, take Via dell'Oriuolo, to reach the historical and topographical Museum Firenze com'era (Florence as it was).

Museum Florence as it was,
Justus Utens, Palazzo Pitti

MUSEUM "FIRENZE COM'ERA" It houses prints, paintings and drawings through which the history of the city unfolds from the XV century to our days.

From Piazza del Duomo, take Via dei Servi leading to Piazza della Santissima Annunziata, bounded by two building fronts with arcades on the sides and dominated by the

CHURCH OF SANTISSIMA ANNUNZIATA Erected in 1250 by the Servants of the Blessed Virgin Mary, this Church was rebuilt between 1444 and 1481 to the design of Michelozzo. A small cloister decorated with frescoes by Baldovinetti, Rosso Fiorentino, Andrea del Sarto and Pontormo introduces the visitor to the church. Though the church underwent several remakes between the XVIII and the XIX centuries, it still features an intact shrine by Michelozzo, aimed at containing the *Annunciation*, deemed to be miraculous. Adjacent to it is the Cloister of the Dead, featuring the fresco of the *Madonna*

Piazza della Santissima
Annunziata

with the Sack (1525), a masterpiece by Andrea del Sarto. Out of the Church, to the left, stand the awesome arcades of the Spedale degli Innocenti, first orphanage to be opened in Europe and also one of the first Renaissance building to be erected. Built to the design of Brunelleschi (1419-26), its volume features nine circular arches built in a clean classical style; the ceramic roundels used to decorate the Spedale facade are by Andrea della Robbia (approximately 1487). Left of the Spedale, through the arch, take via della Colonna, to reach the archaeological museum.

Archaeological Museum,
François Krater

Piazza della Repubblica,
known as Arcone (Large Arch)

ARCHAEOLOGICAL MUSEUM It displays the archaeological collections of Cosimo the Old and Lorenzo the Magnificent, besides interesting Etruscan and Egyptian collections. Especially interesting are the Chimera (Etruscan bronze of the V century B.C.) and the François Vase (an Attic Krater dated VI century B.C.)

PIAZZA DELLA REPUBBLICA Today's square is the result of the urban interventions carried out after Florence had been proclaimed Capital of Italy (1865-71), when medieval towers and churches were destroyed, along with the corporate seats of the Craft Guilds, some palaces owned by noble families, workshops and dwellings. Evidence of what the square looked like before the XIX-century demolitions is provided by prints, paintings and relief-models housed in the topographical museum Firenze com'era. The square stands where the Roman forum used to be, at the crossroad of the "Cardo" and the "Decumanus". This exact spot is marked by a statue by Donatello, still visible in the square.

A large arch with an inscription, reminder of the late XIX century restorations, leads to Via Strozzi and to Via dei Sassetti on the left, leading to Piazza Davanzati, dominated by the sober

PALAZZO DAVANZATI The Palace was built in the mid XIV century, to be purchased by Bernardo Davanzati, a merchant, in 1578. Today it accommodates the Museum of the Old Florentine House. The building is a beautiful XIV-century stately palace, equipped with original furniture and objects of that period.

Palazzo Davanzati,
Hall of Parrots

Upon leaving the Palace, turn left and walk down Porta Rossa, leading to Piazza Santa Trinita. South of this square is the bridge known as Ponte Santa Trinità (Bartolomeo Ammannati 1567-70). By crossing it, the visitor can enjoy an awesome view of both Ponte Vecchio and Ponte dei Lungarni. Looking westwards you will find the

CHURCH OF SANTA TRINITA Built during the second half of the XI century, it was restored in its original shape and style during the second half of the XIV century. Its interior houses the Sassetti Chapel, situated in the right transept and entirely decorated with frescoes by Domenico Ghirlandaio, featuring *Scenes from the life of St Francis* (1483-86); also by him is the beautiful altarpiece with the *Adoration of the Shepherds*.

Upon leaving the Church, on your left, take Via de' Tornabuoni, an elegant street scattered with top designer stores, to find, at the crossroad with Via degli Strozzi, the superb

Church of Santa Trinita, Ghirlandaio,
Adoration of the Shepherds

PALAZZO STROZZI This is one of the most beautiful Renaissance Palaces in Florence. It was built for Filippo Strozzi, a merchant, in 1489, by Benedetto da Maiano in collaboration with Cronaca. Due to the alternating fortunes of the family, the building was left unfinished, missing both the South facade and half its ledge. The Palace is nowadays the seat of the Gabinetto Scientifico Letterario (an Institute for Humanistic Studies), founded in 1819 by Giovan Pietro Vieusseux; it is also equipped with an important international library open to the public. This is also where very interesting temporary exhibitions take place.

From Via Tornabuoni take Via della Vigna Nuova, with its

PALAZZO RUCELLAI The Palace was built for Giovanni Rucellai to the design of Leon Battista Alberti; Bernardo Rossellino erected the building between 1446 and 1451. It is a splendid example of Renaissance civil architecture and today accommodates the Archivi Alinari, a historical photographic enterprise in Florence. Its ground-floor houses the Museum of the history of photography, besides displaying antique photographic equipments. It often hosts temporary exhibitions. Opposite the Palace is the Loggia Rucellai, designed by the same architects who designed the Palace.

Palazzo Strozzi

Palazzo Rucellai

Walking down Via della Vigna Nuova you will reach Piazza Goldoni; turn right into Via dei Fossi, leading to Piazza Santa Maria Novella. This is dominated by the wonderful Church bearing the same name.

CHURCH OF SANTA MARIA NOVELLA The actual church was built between 1279 and 1357 for the Dominican Fathers. Its square was commissioned in 1287 and donated by the authorities to the Dominicans, to serve as a decoration for the church and grant it more prestige. The two white-marble obelisks rest on four bronze tortoises by Giambologna and were used during horse races to mark the start and the finish of the race.

Its marvellous facade, featuring geometrical patterns in white and green marble, was made by Leon Battista Alberti, who designed it in 1470 for Giovanni Rucellai, a local textile merchant.

Its interior houses the choir with frescoes by Ghirlandaio, which the artist made for Giovanni Tornabuoni, in 1485-90, besides those by Orcagna, dating back to the mid XIV century, to be seen in the head-volume of the left transept.

The third bay of the left nave houses a touching fresco by Masaccio, made in 1427, depicting the *Trinity, the Virgin Mary, St John and the Commissioners*.

Just outside the Church is the entrance to the Cloisters, the most beautiful of which is the Green Cloister, built after 1350 and decorated with frescoes by Paolo Uccello, with green as a prevailing colour, hence the name of the Cloister.

Situated at the North side of the Cloister is

Middle nave

the Spanish Chapel, frescoed by Andrea di Bonaiuto approximately in 1355. It was named such for it was destined to the religious services of the Spanish retinue of Eleonora of Toledo, wife of Cosmo I de'Medici.

Giotto, wooden Crucifix

Tornabuoni Chapel,
Domenico Ghirlandaio,
Visitation

Masaccio, Holy Trinity

Spanish Chapel, Andrea di Bonaiuto,
Church Militant and Church Triumphant

Piazzale Michelangelo

NEARBY:

PIAZZALE MICHELANGELO The square offers one of the most beautiful and famous views worldwide. It was designed by Architect Giuseppe Poggi (1860-75); in the centre of the piazza stands a copy of Michelangelo's *David*, surrounded by other copies featuring statues of the the *Medicean Tombs* of San Lorenzo. Not too far from the square, a staircase leads to the Church of San Salvatore al Monte. Designed by Cronaca in 1499, it is also known as "la bella villanella", as Michelangelo used to call it.

From Viale Galileo a monumental staircase takes you to the

CHURCH OF SAN MINIATO AL MONTE Started in 1018 and finished at the beginning of the XIII century, this Church is one of the finest Romanesque buildings in Florence. Particularly significant is the chromatic contrast between the white and green marble stripes, used for the marvellous geometrically patterned facade, built in 1090.

Its interior, restored in the mid XIX century, features a balustrade in inlaid marble and a pulpit of the XIII century. It also houses an apsidal mosaic dating back to the same period.

Church of San Miniato, mosaic on the facade

The central nave also features the *Crucifix Chapel* by Michelozzo (1448), decorated by Luca della Robbia; in the left nave there is the *Chapel of the Cardinal of Portugal*, designed by Antonio Manetti and housing the *tomb of Jacopo di Lusitania, Archbishop of Lisbon*, made by Rossellino (1461). The ceiling medallions are by Luca della Robbia.

Apsidal mosaic, Christ Pantocrator among the Virgin Mary, San Miniato and the symbols of the four Evangelists

Benedetto di Buglione (*attr.*) San Miniato, glazed terracotta

Luca della Robbia (*attr.*), Crucifix in glazed terracotta

Sacristy with a cycle of frescoes by Spinello Aretino and the benches by Jacopo Monciatti

CHARTERHOUSE AT GALLUZZO This monumental complex is situated in the suburb of Galluzzo, South of Florence. Founded by Niccolò Acciaiuoli, a powerful Florentine politician, it was started in 1341 and benefited from several donations. In 1958, it was taken over by the Cistercians monks. The *Palazzo degli Studi*, with its raw stone exterior and its gothic single lancet windows, accommodates the Art Gallery. The facade of the Church of San Lorenzo was built to the design of Luca Fancelli (1556). Its underground chapels house the superb ground-level *tomb of Cardinal Agnolo Acciaiuoli*, probably by Francesco da Sangallo (circa 1556). Besides this, the place houses three more ground-level tombstones, considered to be masterpieces, namely the *tomb of Acciaiuolo*, father of Niccolò Acciaiuoli, that of Lorenzo (†1353), son of Niccolò, and that of his sister Lapa. Worth visiting is also the Monastery, dominated by the Great Cloister (1498 -1516), with the annexed Friars' cells, which stand out among the highest expressions of Renaissance architecture.

Charterhouse at Galluzzo

FIESOLE Situated atop a hill dominating the Arno and the Mugnone Valley, 8 km North of Florence, it can be easily reached by bus, leaving from Florence city centre, or by car. First evidence of its Etruscan origins dates back to the VII-VI century B.C. In 90 B.C., Porzio Catone punished it for taking the field against Rome, and, in 80 B.C., Silla conquered it. This is how *Faesulae* fell under the Roman rule. After Florence was founded and after the barbaric invasions, Fiesole's power declined and the town eventually succumbed to Florence in 1125. Its archaeological park includes the remains of both the Etruscan and the Roman periods, such as the beautiful Roman amphitheatre, containing 3,000 people. Built in the first century B.C., it still houses beautiful theatre representations at summer time. The park also includes a Museum, displaying the archaeological finds from the excavations. Among the ruins are the thermal baths, also dating back to the beginning of the Imperial period, with their sequence of rooms that are still visible. Also visible are the ruins of the Etruscan walls, dating back to the IV century B. C. From Fiesole central square, Piazza Mino da Fiesole, built on the ancient Roman Forum, the visitor can access the cathedral (St Romolo's). Built in 1028 by Bishop Jacopo the Bavarian, it underwent radical restoration works at the end of the XIX century. Its facade was entirely rebuilt and its bell tower dates back to 1213. Its interior still features the structure of a Romanesque basilica. At

Roman Theatre

Cathedral of San Romolo

the margins of the square, behind the Monument featuring the *Meeting at Teano* by O. Calzolari (1906), there is the XIV-century Praetorian Palace, reworked both in the XV and in the XVI centuries. On the right side lies the Oratory of Santa Maria Primerana, with its XVI-century arcades. Opposite the Oratory, on the right, stands the Bishop's Palace, built in the XI century and reconstructed in 1675. From this square, Via di San Francesco, will take you to a small hill, where the Etruscan and the Roman acropolises used to be. This was also the location of a medieval fortress, which the Florentines pulled down in 1125. Situated in a suggestive landscape, the Church of San Francesco was founded in 1330, built as an oratory for the Florentine hermit nuns, it was taken over by the Franciscan Monks in 1407, who enlarged it. It underwent questionable restoration works at the beginning of the XX century.

Fiesole, Church and Monastery of San Francesco

SAN DOMENICO On leaving Fiesole, on the road to Florence, lies the hamlet of San Domenico, hosting a monastery built between 1405 and 1406, where Friar Giovanni da Fiesole, mainly known as Beato Angelico (approximately 1395-1455), embraced the religious life. For this monastery he produced the fresco with the *Blessing Madonna*, later repainted. The restoration works, carried out in 1960, enabled the sinopite to surface once again. He also frescoed a big *Crucifix* for the Chapter Hall. On the orders of Napoleon, the religious orders were suppressed and the friars were dispossessed. Even though they succeeded in buying the monastery again, they had to sell two of Beato Angelico's frescoes. Annexed to the monastery is the Church, the construction works of which started in 1406 and were only completed in 1635, with the completion of an outside arcade and an elegant bell tower (Matteo Nigetti). The Church houses a panel from the triptych of the main altar, once again by Beato Angelico.

San Domenico, Church and Monastery

San Domenico, Beato Angelico, Crucifix

BADIA FIESOLANA Upon leaving San Domenico, take Via di Badia dei Roccettini, to reach the Abbey of Fiesole, the hamlet's Cathedral up to 1026. Destroyed, it was rebuilt by the Camaldolese monks together with the Monastery and was dedicated to San Bartolomeo. It was then taken over by the Benedictines from Cassino up to 1439, then by the Canons Regular of St Augustine, referred to as Roccettini since the beginning of the XIX century. From 1456 the Abbey was under the protection of Cosimo the Old, who enlarged it. Unfortunately, upon his death in 1464, works stopped and its facade was left unfinished, leaving only a small Romanesque facade in the middle (XII century), covered in white and green marble, in the same style as the Baptistery (see page 12).

Badia Fiesolana

The one-nave interior with its side chapels is in the style of Brunelleschi (1461-64); even though the architect never worked at it, he apparently suggested its design.

MORE TO SEE OUTSIDE FLORENCE

Certaldo

CERTALDO The town historical centre is situated on a hilltop surrounded by walls, known as "il Castello", made up entirely with characteristic red bricks, used both for raising the buildings and for the streets. Its modern portion, "il Borgo", is situated downhill. It belonged to the Counts Alberti in ancient times, but, in 1293, it was permanently taken over by Florence. An illustrious citizen of Certaldo was Giovanni Boccaccio (1313-1373), who spent here the last years of his life. Also worth visiting is *Boccaccio's House*, that is, however, a XV-century building, hence the famous writer could never have lived there. He probably lived in the house next to that one instead, that was destroyed during the last war. However, it is a beautiful building, featuring a tower and a loggia, today accommodating the "National Centre of Studies on Boccaccio". The CHURCH OF SANTI MICHELE AND JACOPO is a XIII-century building, restored at the beginning of the XX century. It houses Boccaccio's mortal remains, kept in a XVI-century cenotaph, decorated with a bust by Giovanni Francesco Rustici (1503), also bearing an epitaph by Coluccio Salutati. Its tombstone is by the sculptor Mario Moschi (1954). The PRAETORIAN PALACE or PALAZZO DEL VICARIO, originally the residence of the Counts Alberti, became the residence of the podestàs and vicars of Florence from 1293. The actual palace is a XV-century remake and features a facade decorated with the coat of arms of the vicars in stone and enamelled terracotta. Its houses frescoes and fragments of these, dating back to the XV and XVI centuries.

CHIANTI This is the name of the hilly landscape area in the heart of Tuscany, situated between Florence and Siena. It is famous worldwide for the prestigious Chianti wine that is produced here. It is undoubtedly one of the most suggestive landscapes of the region, scattered with wonderful castles (the Castle of Broglio: owned by the Ricasolis since 1167; the XIII-century Castle of Meleto), monasteries (the Badia a Coltibuono, a XI-century Abbey), ancient hamlets (Castellina in Chianti, Radda in Chianti, Gaiole in Chianti, Montefioralle, hometown of the Vespucci family, where the celebrated navigator Amerigo Vespucci was born), along with typical wineries with their awesome vineyards. GREVE, one of the most famous places in the Chianti region, is located here, at about 30 km from Florence. It was named after an ancient castle, burnt in 1325 by Commander Castruccio Castracani. In the heart of this town, Piazza Matteotti, there is a peculiar asymmetrical square bounded by arcades and terraces. Each year, during the third week of September, Greve holds the Chianti Classico Wine Festival; moreover, visitors can taste this wine throughout the whole year, in the many shops selling local wines.

Chianti, Badia a Coltibuono

Empoli, Collegiate Church of Sant'Andrea

EMPOLI The town was raised after 1119, all around the parish church of Sant'Andrea and, in 1182, swore allegiance to the Commune of Florence. It is nowadays famous for its glass industry. Worth visiting is the COLLEGIATE CHURCH OF SANT'ANDREA, featuring a magnificent facade, dating back to 1093. It was built in a Florentine Romanesque style, with white and green marble (the lower portion is still part of the original facade, whereas the upper portion is a 1736 remake). The XVIII-century interior, shaped in the form of an Egyptian cross, was extensively modified, just like the bell tower was, after the destruction suffered in 1944. Also worth visiting is the annexed MUSEUM, housing several artworks by Renaissance authors, among which is the *Annunciation* by Bernardo Rossellino, a *Virgin Mary and Child* by Filippo Lippi and the *Pietà*, a masterpiece by Masolino

(1425), besides a marble baptismal font, sculptured in 1447, in the style of Donatello. The Church of Santo Stefano, built by the Augustinians in the XIV century, houses fragments of frescoes by Masolino, dating back to 1424.

MONTESENARIO Past the holiday resort of Bivigliano, a winding road will take you to Mount Senario (m. 815), on top of which there is a monastery founded in 1234, by a group of seven Florentine noblemen, who, maybe the year before, had retired from the world to live as hermits in some of the grottoes of that mountain. These were the founders of the *Servite Friars*, who restored their monastery in 1594. Visitors can enjoy a beautiful panoramic view of the surrounding valleys and have a taste of the liquor the friars still produce in the traditional way in their little pantry. The *Servite Friars* are also in Florence, in the Church of Santissima Annunziata (page 36).

Montesenario

MUGELLO This valley is situated North-East of Florence, unfolding between the Apennine and the two rivers, the Arno and the Sieve rivers. Though the landscape is varied, it is mainly mild hilly. Among the most important towns in the Sieve valley is BORGO SAN LORENZO, originally owned by the Bishops of Florence since the X century, it passed under the direct domination of Florence in 1290. Due to frequent earthquakes, among which is the most destructive 1919 earthquake, little is left of its medieval past. Another well known town is VICCHIO, which was enlarged over the centuries within the walls the Florentines erected in 1324. This is where the famous Friar Giovanni, known as Beato Angelico (approximately 1395-1455) was born, whereas the great painter GIOTTO (1267-1337) was born in the hamlet of VESPIGNANO, a few kilometres away from Vicchio. His restored house has nowadays become a small museum. Another must-see of Mugello is SCARPERIA: founded by the Florentines in 1306, it became the seat of the Vicarage in 1415. Its Praetorian Palace, also known as the Vicar's Palace, built in 1306, is made up of a central volume and a tower, crowned with Guelph battlements. Its facade is partially covered up with the stone and majolica coat of arms of vicars. Opposite the Palace is the Provostship, housing XV- and XVI-century artworks. Scarperia is famous for both its craft- and industrial production of knives. The area of Mugello also includes the VILLA MEDICEA DI CAFAGGIOLO, a crenellated fortress with tower and galleries that was Lorenzo the Magnificent's favourite place to be, for he loved to go hunting there. Last but not least is the CASTELLO DEL TREBBIO, a castle built in 1427-1436 by Michelozzo, for Cosimo the Old.

Vespignano, Giotto's House

Scarperia, Town Hall

VALLOMBROSA This is a holiday resort built around an ancient monastery on Mount Secchieta, one of the mountains of the Pratomagno massif, surrounded by a secular fir-wood and by a forest of firs, chestnut-trees and beeches. In 1208, Giovanni Gualberto of the Florentine Visdomini family took refuge with a comrade of his in these woods, where he lived as a hermit, thus renouncing to all worldly affairs and pleasures. This is how the *Benedictine Congregation of Vallombrosa* was founded. Acknowledged in 1055 by Pope Vittore II, they were originally a congregation which made profession of poverty, but later became rich and powerful, to the extent that they could build an abbey, as grand as to resemble a fortress.

Vallombrosa, Monastery

The actual monastery dates back to the XV century and underwent modifications and enlargements during the XVI and the XVII centuries, in order to meet with the needs of an ever richer and more powerful monastic order.

VINCI is a small hamlet situated on a hill richly planted in vine-yards and olive groves, also featuring extensive works of terrac-ing, supported by the characteristic *dry-stone walls*. Famous for being Leonardo's hometown (1452-1519), the town was erect-ed around the castle owned by the Counts Guidi (XII century), that was restored in 1952. The Castle and the Palazzina Uzielli accommodate LEONARDO'S MUSEUM, displaying a rich collec-tion of wood models, reproducing the extraordinary machines invented by Leonardo Da Vinci. Such models feature, among others, machines to fly and weave, clocks, war instruments, hy-draulic projects. The castle also accommodates LEONARDO'S LIBRARY, that is also an important research and documentation centre for studies on Leonardo's work. Since 1993 a new ex-hibition hall has been opened to the public, housed in the cas-tle basement: LEONARDO DA VINCI'S IDEAL MUSEUM, displaying works and documents with their ancient originals, along with

on the right:
Museum of Leonardo da Vinci

below:
Turin Royal Library,
Leonardo da Vinci,
self-portrait

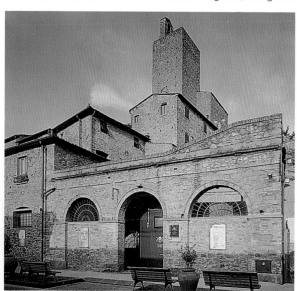

over 50 models reproducing Leonardo's designs. With the nascent project "Giardino di Leonardo e dell'Utopia", the Ideal Museum is building an open-air thematic museum.

Vinci, Leonardo's Museum, Castle of the Counts Guidi, Models in the section dedicated to Mechanisms and Instruments

Vinci, Leonardo's Museum, Castle of the Counts Guidi, model of a bicycle

Vinci, Leonardo's Museum, Castle of the Counts Guidi, gallery with sections dedicated to Flight, Mechanisms and Instruments

Vinci, Leonardo da Vinci's Ideal Museum, Motor coach referred to as *car*

Vinci, Leonardo da Vinci's Ideal Museum, Floats to walk on the water surface

Vinci, Leonardo da Vinci's Ideal Museum, Screw steering gear

itinerary

2

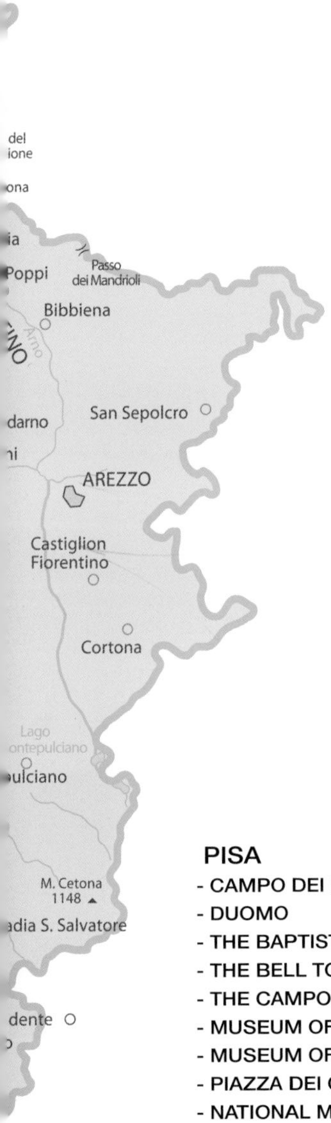

del
ione

ona

ia

Poppi
Passo
dei Mandrioli

Bibbiena

San Sepolcro

AREZZO

Castiglion
Fiorentino

Cortona

Lago
ontepulciano

ulciano

M. Cetona
1148

adia S. Salvatore

dente

darno

ni

PISA

The city is situated 10 km away from the sea, north of the lagoon, on the mouths of the rivers Arno and Serchio. The Etruscans, who inhabited this area since the V Century B.C., probably gave the city the name of Pisa (meaning mouth in their language), upon expanding to the North. The city was a Roman military colony, known as *Julia Obse Quens*, under the rule of Cesare Ottaviano, who restored the *Portus Pisanus*. Already under the Romans, during the Gothic times and under the Lombards, it became a prominent base for naval expeditions, whereas, under the Carolingians, it stood out for defending the Tyrrhenian coasts from the Saracens incursions. From the XI century onwards, Pisa became a commune and its power grew, thanks to its trading businesses in the Mediterranean. Along with Genoa, its dominion expanded to reach Sardinia, where it contributed to freeing the island from the Saracens (1015-16). The XII century was a glorious one for the Pisans: besides being a maritime power both militarily and as a commercial centre, Pisa reached its maximum splendour even artistically between the end of 1200 and the beginning of 1300, when also becoming a maritime Republic. Its military decline

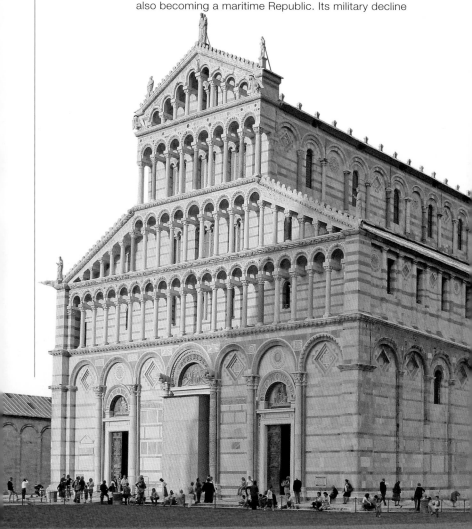

started soon though, when the Pisan army was defeated by the Genoeses in Meloria, on August 6, 1284, and Pisa almost lost its entire fleet. At the same time, internal struggles caused the Ghibelline faction to weaken, rendering it an easy prey to the dominion of the Gambacorta Seigneurs. After a few years of alternating fortunes, Pisa, that had lost its Tyrrhenian dominions in the meanwhile, lost its independence and power. After a long siege, in 1406, Florence defeated the Republic. The city started to flourish again thanks to Lorenzo the Magnificent, who reformed the already existing "Studio", founded in the XII century, and, in 1472, started to build the seat of the "Sapienza", also known as University Institute of Studies. Under the Medicean Grand Duchy, Pisa developed to the extent that, in 1562, Cosimo I chose it as the seat of the Military Order of St Stephen's knights. Under the rule of the House of Lorraine, Pisa could maintain an important role and stayed a lively city, spurred by the further development of the University. In 1860, it was annexed to the rising Kingdom of Italy by a plebiscite. It was severely hit by bombings during the years of World War II (1940-45), with devastating damage of public and private heritage. It is currently one of the most visited tourist resorts in Italy, as well as a prestigious university centre.

Campo dei Miracoli
also known as Piazza del Duomo

CAMPO DEI MIRACOLI also known as PIAZZA DEL DUOMO. The square is the artistic and religious heart of the city. Surrounded by the mid XII-century crenellated walls at its North and East borders, it is overlooked by the DUOMO, the highest expression of Pisa Romanesque style.

Campo dei Miracoli

Duomo, facade

Giovanni Pisano, pulpit

DUOMO (Cathedral of Santa Maria Assunta) Built by Buscheto in 1064, the Cathedral was consecrated when still unfinished, in 1118, by Pope Gelasio II. At the end of the XII century, Rainaldo erected its facade, featuring Buscheto's sarcophagus in the first blind arch on the left. Its external decorations are extraordinary; it took two centuries to complete them.

The building features a striped pattern, in white and black marbles, with blind arcades, small galleries and pilaster strips. It also features fine marble mosaics and oriental-style enamelled glass tesseras. The transept section overlooking the bell tower includes the bronze *Door of San Ranieri* (main entrance to the Cathedral), cast by Bonanno Pisano in 1180, depicting the *Scenes from the Life of Our Saviour*. At the crossing of the two wings of the church rises an ovoidal dome, surrounded by a gothic open gallery, added in 1380. Its Latin-cross plan with five naves features a triple-nave transept and a wide apse. Over the middle nave is the women's gallery (situated above the side naves and overlooking the central one; in early Christian basilicas, as well as in a large number of medieval churches, this gallery was only reserved to women), also unfolding in the transept. The panelled ceiling was reworked after 1595 (following a fire).

The church is like a casket, housing several works of art, among which the most famous is the *Pulpit* by Giovanni Pisano (1302-11): its hexagonal structure rests on a round pedestal with inscriptions. Its eleven supports, some of which are columns, rest on bases or statues of lions. It is considered a masterpiece of the Italian gothic sculptural tradition.

The pulpit was disassembled in 1599 and reassembled in 1926, due to reconstruction works of the portions that had been irreparably damaged.

In the middle of the central nave hangs the famous 1587 bronze chandelier, known as *Galileo's Lamp*; it is traditionally believed that the scientist used to watch it sway ("*And yet it moves*").

The DOME features frescoes by Orazio and Giro-lamo Riminaldi (1631) and the floor below (XIII century) is a Cosmatesque marble floor (from the name of the marble craftsmen, the Cosmatis, working in Rome and Lazio as decorators and architects, between the beginning of the XII and the end of the XIII century. They used white and coloured marble, porphyry, serpentine-stone tesseras for their decorations, but also resorted to glass and gold tesseras).

Baptistery

THE BAPTISTERY

It is situated opposite the Cathedral and features a circular plan, surmounted by a pyramidal dome. Its construction started in 1152, under the direction of Architect Diotisalvi.

From 1260, Nicola Pisano supervised the works, whereas his son Giovanni Pisano started to work at its external decoration in 1284. The dome was designed in 1358, but was only completed at the end of the century. The Baptistery accommodates the famous *Pulpit* by Nicola Pisano (1260), featuring an hexagonal plan with seven columns, partially resting on lions. The central column rests on sculptures of talamons and animals; on the columns rest trefoil gothic arches, that, together with the corner pillars, provide a support to the bulwark. It is one of the most beautiful works of the Tuscan Romanesque period.

Nicola Pisano, pulpit

Bell Tower also known as the Leaning Tower

THE BELL TOWER

also known as THE LEANING TOWER
Due to the loose substrate of sand silt in Piazza dei Miracoli, all the buildings that have been erected there tend to lean, though none of them is leaning as much as the famous "*Leaning Tower*".

Besides being an extraordinarily beautiful bell tower, it is also a standing miracle. Construction of the tower started in August 1173, according to Vasari, to the design of Bonanno Pisano, and progressed to the third floor, when a sudden subsidence of the soil caused all works to be halted, only to be resumed in 1275, by Giovanni di Simone, who tried to compensate its tilt. It was only between 1350 and 1372 that the magnificent tower was finally completed with the construction of the bell chamber, featuring a diameter measuring less than that of the tower itself, perhaps by Tommaso Pisano. Its overall height measures 54.5 metres. The circular tower, entirely covered in white marble, features blind arches resting on semi-columns at the first floor, and six orders of small balconies, also resting on columns. Its interior, shaped as a big telescope, features a flight of 294 steps unfolding in a spiral flow, all around an empty core nucleus; each floor is provided with an exit on the corresponding external ring-shaped gallery, so as to enjoy the awesome view.

The last floor opens onto the roof terrace, also featuring a bell chamber, housing seven bells dating back to the XVII – XIX centuries. This is also the place where Galileo Galilei performed his first experiments about gravity.

Camposanto

Museum of the Opera del
Duomo, unknown author,
small panel depicting St John
the Evangelist

THE CAMPOSANTO This monumental cemetery is situated on the north-side of the square. Its construction commenced in 1277 by Giovanni di Simone, meant to surround the lawn of the ancient cemetery where, legend has it, Archbishop Ubaldo de'Lanfranchi had brought a shipload of sacred soil from Golgotha, in 1203, shipped on the Pisan vessels. The cloister has a rectangular structure with an internal gallery that opens onto the lawn, still housing the tombs of famous Pisans and fragments of superb XIV-century frescoes, unfortunately damaged by the bombings of the evening of July 27, 1944.

THE MUSEUM OF THE OPERA DEL DUOMO Situated in Piazza del Duomo, this museum is accommodated in the former Chapter Hall of the XIII-century Cathedral. It was opened in 1986 to store the finds and works that were once displayed in both the Cathedral and the Baptistery: worth seeing are the ivory *Virgin Mary with Child* by Giovanni Pisano (1300) and an Islamic *Hippogriff* (half horse and half griffon), which the Pisans stole during their battles against the Saracens.

MUSEUM OF THE SINOPITES Situated in Piazza del Duomo, this museum accommodates the preparatory drawings (sinopites) for the frescoes of the Camposanto, that remained unaltered, despite the fall of colour after the bombings of July 27, 1944. Therefore, they were detached from the Camposanto walls, restored and displayed in this museum, also housing works by artists like Andrea Bonaiuti, Antonio Veneziano, Taddeo Gaddi and Benozzo Gozzoli.

PIAZZA DEI CAVALIERI This square was the ancient heart of the Republican city, transformed by Vasari to accommodate the seat of the *Order of St Stephen's knights*, founded by Cosimo I, in 1561, and chiefly aimed at fighting pirate raids in the Mediterranean. On the right side of the square stands the CHURCH OF SANTO STEFANO DEI CAVALIERI, designed by Vasari (1565-69) and featuring a facade by Giovanni de'Medici (1594-1606). The bell tower is also by Vasari

Church of Santo Stefano
dei Cavalieri

(1570-72). On the left-hand side of the church stands the PALAZZO DEI CAVALIERI (Knights' Palace), resulting from a radical restoration by Vasari (1562) of the former *Palace of the Elders*, some ruins of which are still visible. Its facade is decorated with graffito works and busts depicting six famous Grand Dukes of Tuscany (from Cosimo I to Cosimo III). The palace, erected to house the headquarters of the Knights of St Stephen's Order, is nowadays the seat of the *Scuola Normale Superiore*, a University Institute for the advanced study of liberal arts, philosophy, mathematics and sciences. Opposite the palace there is the *Equestrian Monument of Cosimo I*, and the beautiful *fountain* by Pietro Francavilla (1596). Also in this square is the PALAZZO DELL'OROLOGIO, later known as the Gherardesca Palace, a fine architectural and urban-planning solution by Vasari, that was, however, erected after his death, in 1607, always for the Knights of St Stephen. This building was erected with the remains of both the *Torre delle Sette Vie*, a former jail of Pisa, and the *Torre dei Gualandi*, also known as the *Tower of mew* first and as the *Tower of hunger* afterward, due to the famous episode Dante wrote about in his Inferno, telling of Count Ugolino della Gherardesca's imprisonment and death; the latter was actually jailed here with his offspring.

NATIONAL MUSEUM OF SAN MATTEO (Lungarno Mediceo, Piazza San Matteo) It displays a valuable collection of Florentine and Pisan works of art of the Tuscan school, ranging from the XII to the XV century. Among these are: the *Madonna with Child and Saints* (polyptych) by Simone Martini (1319), *Our Lady of Milk* by Nino Pisano and *St Paul* by Masaccio (from the dismantled polyptych of the Church of Santa Maria del Carmine).

CHURCH OF SANTA MARIA DELLA SPINA (Lungarno Gambacorti) A jewel of the Pisan Gothic art, this Church is situated on the river bank. It was originally erected to be a small oratory dedicated to Santa Maria di Pontenovo. It was restored in 1323 and consecrated to accommodate a *thorn* from Jesus Christ's crown. When, in 1871, the stability of the building became precarious, due to water infiltrations, the church was dismantled and reassembled in the actual location along the banks of the river Arno.

Church of Santa Maria della Spina

CHURCH OF SAN PAOLO A RIPA D'ARNO (Piazza San Paolo a Ripa d'Arno) The first nucleus of this structure dates back to 805. It was later rebuilt between the XI and the XII century, in the same Romanesque style of the Cathedral, and consecrated in 1148 by Pope Eugene III. The church was severely damaged, due to the bombings in 1943, following which, it was entirely rebuilt.

ABBEY OF SAN PIETRO A GRADO It was erected in the XI century, on the site where, back to Roman times, the farthest ferry slip on the river Arno laid; legend has it that St Peter landed here. The majestic church was built in Livorno tufa and white and black marbles of San Giuliano. It features a magnificent interior, shaped like a basilica, with three trussed naves. The walls of the central nave are decorated with a cycle of frescoes, dating back to the beginning of the XIV century, probably by Deodato Orlandi.

Abbey of San Pietro a Grado

Abbey of San Pietro a Grado, interior

SAN MINIATO Situated on a hill dominating the plane of lower Valdarno, the town was built on the ancient Roman Quarto and developed from the VIII century onwards. It was the seat of Imperial Vicars, among which was Boniface, father of Countess Matilda. Also many emperors of the Holy Roman Empire lived here; among these are Barbarossa (1178) and Frederick II, who, in 1240, built the Fortress.

San Miniato

This is why it was called San Miniato al Tedesco. In 1347, the town was under the dominion of Florence, against which it rebelled in 1367, only to be re-conquered two years afterwards; from 1369 onwards, despite its attempts to rebel, San Miniato remained under the authority of Florence, following the whereabouts of its political events.

DUOMO (Piazza del Duomo) Dedicated to the Virgin Mary of Assumption and to San Genesio, it was originally built in the XIII century and rebuilt several times, then restored in 1860. It still maintains a very original decoration in XIII-century majolicas. Its bell tower is known as *Matilde's Tower*, in honour of Countess Matilda who was born here (1046-1115). It is the only remainder of the ancient fortifications. Its Latin-cross, triple-nave interior was decorated in the XVIII and XIX centuries and houses some interesting Tombs, besides valuable works of art, among which is its superb ceiling.

San Miniato, Duomo

DIOCESAN MUSEUM (adjacent to the Cathedral) This museum houses some valuable works of art, such as the *Crucifixion* by Filippo Lippi, the *Madonna of the Belt and Saints*, probably by Andrea del Castagno, and Our *Saviour*, a terracotta by Andrea del Verrocchio.

CHURCH OF SAN FRANCESCO (East of Piazza del Duomo) Rebuilt in bricks in 1276 and restored in 1404, it was completed in 1480. The church was erected on a pre-existing small temple dedicated to San Miniato. Its interior still displays traces of a XV-century fresco from Masolino's fresco school.

CHURCH OF SAN DOMENICO (Piazza del Popolo) The church is actually dedicated to *Santi Jacopo and Lucia de Foris Portam*. Rebuilt after 1330 and reworked in the XVII and in the XVIII centuries, it still preserves its original facade. Its single-nave interior houses the marble tomb of Giovanni Chellini by Bernardo Rossellino, made in 1462 to the design of Donatello. The Spedalinghi Chapel was restored and frescoed in 1900 by G. Chini.

PALAZZO DEI VICARI It was built in the XII century, encompassing the remains of the ancient castle that was the seat of the imperial vicars.

THE TOWN HALL It was built in the XIV century as the Palace of the Lords of San Miniato. The Council Hall houses the *Madonna with Child among the allegories of the Cardinal and Theological virtues*, a fresco by Cenni di Francesco. The ground floor accommodates the oratory of the Virgin Mary of Loreto, featuring walls with frescoes dating back to both the end of 1300 and the beginning of 1400, and an altar surmounted by a majestic wooden altarpiece of the 1500 Florentine school.

THE FORTRESS This is what is left of the ancient building erected for Frederick II (1194-1250) in the XIII century. The place offers an awesome view over the Arno Valley.

Volterra coat of arms,
Florence,Cappella dei Principi

VOLTERRA Situated, like many Etruscan towns, on a plateau, it was first a very important Villanovian centre (IX-VIII century B.C.), then became the seat of an Etruscan Lucumonie, a Roman Municipality and, from the V century A.D., it was made an Episcopal seat.

It was under the dominion of the Pannocchieschi family (1150-1239) until it passed under that of Florence (1361).

In more recent times the town shared the same fate of both the Medicean Duchy and the Grand Duchy of Tuscany.

Besides being famous for its museums, Volterra is also renowned for its alabaster artefacts.

The Fortress

Porta dell'Arco *(Etruscan Arch)*

THE FORTRESS It dominates the hill of Volterra and is made of the XIV-century Old Fortress and of the XV-century New Fortress, joined one to the other and both modified for Lorenzo the Magnificent after 1472. This is one of the most imposing and well preserved stronghold of all Florentine Renaissance architecture.

The two fortresses have mainly served as dungeons, even today they accommodate a top-security prison and are, therefore, closed to the public.

PORTA DELL'ARCO also knows as ETRUSCAN ARCH. This gate is part of the Etruscan city walls and still preserves its original external door frames (IV-III century B.C.), whereas its archivolt dates back to the Roman period. The door is made of large blocks of tufa, laid edge to edge without the use of mortar. On the key brick as well as on the two bases, the arch still features three human heads carved in stone, a reminder, perhaps, of the Eastern practice of displaying the cut-off heads of enemies on the city walls, as a warning for the others.

PIAZZA DEI PRIORI This is one among the most beautiful medieval squares in Italy, also offering a beautiful view. It is overlooked by the PALAZZO DEI PRIORI. Construction of this public palace started in 1208 and finished in 1254, probably making it one of the most ancient in Italy. Its facade is decorated with the terracotta coat-of-arms of the Florentine superintendents of the XV-XVI centuries. The palace is also surmounted by a pentagonal tower, the edge of which was built in 1846. Today it is the seat of the town administration offices.

Palazzo dei Priori,
Hall of the Council

Palazzo dei Priori, facade,
coat of arms of the
Superintendents

DUOMO (Piazza San Giovanni) This cathedral was rebuilt around 1120 on a pre-existing church. According to Vasari, Nicola Pisano enlarged and decorated it in the XIII century.

Even though its structure maintains a Romanesque Latin-cross plan, its three naves show a late Renaissance taste, almost certainly due to the repeated remakes that followed over the centuries.

Its interior houses some remarkable works, such as the *Deposition* (2nd chapel of the transept), a masterpiece of the Romanesque wood carving production of the XIII century, and the *Pulpit*, dating back to 1584, featuring sculptured reliefs of the XII and the XIII centuries, by sculptors of the celebrated school of Guglielmo Pisano. Also on display here are the magnificent *Annunciation* by Friar Bartolomeo (1497) and the XV-century *Epiphany*, in enamelled terracotta, made by Zaccaria Zocchi.

Volterra, Duomo,
Pupils of Giovanni Pisano, Pulpit

Mariotto Albertinelli, Annunciation

Unknown author,
XIII-century Deposition, polychrome wood

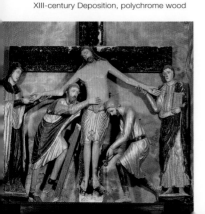

DIOCESAN MUSEUM OF SACRED ART (Via Romana)

Accommodated in the Bishop's Palace, it displays an important collection of sculptures and architectural fragments from the Cathedral, besides a number of vestments, miniated manuscripts and silverware. Among these are: the *Bust of San Lino*, Saint Patron of Volterra, a terracotta dated to the XV century by Giovanni della Robbia, the *Bust of San Ottaviano*, in chiselled silver, by Antonio del Pollaiolo, and *Christ Crucified*, in golden bronze, by Giambologna.

Diocesan Museum of Sacred Art, Antonio del Pollaiolo, Bust of St Ottaviano

Volterra, Diocesan Museum of Sacred Art, Rosso Fiorentino, Madonna on the Throne between St John the Baptist and St Bartholomew

Diocesan Museum of Sacred Art, miniated Chorale book (1508-1510)

Diocesan Museum of Sacred Art, Giovanni della Robbia, Bust of St Lino

Diocesan Museum of Sacred Art, Giambologna, Christ crucified

Diocesan Museum of Sacred Art, alabaster Ciborium (1574) reproducing the Temple of Bramante in San Pietro in Montorio, Rome

Volterra
Town Art Gallery,
Room XI

ART GALLERY AND CIVIC MUSEUM (Via dei Sarti) Accommodated in the Minucci-Solaini Palace, it houses a large collection of paintings; many are the works by Florentine artists, such as the *Majesty of Christ*, painted in 1492 by Ghirlandaio, the *Deposition* by Rosso Fiorentino, a mannerist work of art dated 1521, besides the *Annunciation* and the *Madonna with Child and Saints*, both famous works by Luca Signorelli (1491).

Town Art Gallery,
Luca Signorelli, Madonna
with Child and Saints

next page:
Town Art Gallery,
Rosso Fiorentino,
Deposition from the Cross

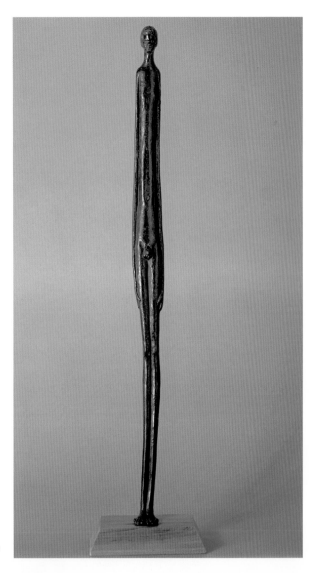

Volterra
Guarnacci Etruscan Museum,
Evening Shadow

GUARNACCI ETRUSCAN MUSEUM (Via Don Minzoni) It displays the most relevant collection of Etruscan urns worldwide. This collection was put together after the finds in 1731 by the Canon of Volterra Cathedral, Pietro Franceschini, who donated them to the town of Volterra the following year.

In 1761, Abbot Mario Guarnacci (1701-1785), who promoted several archaeological excavations, donated his entire collection to the museum. One of the most remarkable works on display here is the small votive bronze statue known as the *Evening Shadow*, as Gabriele d'Annunzio called it, for it reminded him of a person's shadow projected in the evening light. The small statue was found by a peasant in 1879, and used as a poker for the fire, until, by pure chance, someone recognised it as a masterpiece of Etruscan art. Among the works housed here, particularly remarkable are: the *vase with black figures*, the *cinerary urn with the deceased (Atteone)*, the *mirror with dioscuri* and the *Urn of the spouses*.

Vase with black figures

Cinerary Urn with the defunct
known as Atteone

Mirror with Dioscuri

Alabaster and tufa
vases and cinerary urns

Urn of the Spouses

OTHER PLACES IN THE SURROUNDINGS OF PISA

LARDERELLO This town became famous thanks to the boracic industry, powered by the fumaroles; it was named after the French Francesco de Larderel, who, in 1818, started to extract boric acid from the so-called "lagoni" of Montecerboli. Discovered in 1777 by the German chemist Francesco Hofer, boric acid was commercialised by De Larderel, who installed the first factory, which Leopold II called Larderello in 1846. It was thanks to Prince Piero Ginori Conti that, in 1905, the energy from the fumaroles was used to create electric power. Today, it produces 10% of the power used in one million houses in Italy.

Larderello, Fumaroles

TENUTA DI SAN ROSSORE This awesome natural park unfolds over an area of 3,000 hectares, mainly covered with woods that stretch from the river Serchio to the River Arno. It

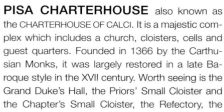

was used as a hunting lodge by the Medici family, before becoming a property of the House of Lorraine and of the House of Savoy. After the fall of the monarchy, it became the *Presidential summer residence*.

PISA CHARTERHOUSE also known as the CHARTERHOUSE OF CALCI. It is a majestic complex which includes a church, cloisters, cells and guest quarters. Founded in 1366 by the Carthusian Monks, it was largely restored in a late Baroque style in the XVII century. Worth seeing is the Grand Duke's Hall, the Priors' Small Cloister and the Chapter's Small Cloister, the Refectory, the

Tenuta di San Rossore

Chapter's Chapel, the Large Cloister and the Church. It currently accommodates the *Museum of natural history and of the territory* of the University of Pisa, displaying paleontological collections, collections of minerals, along with zoological collections.

Pisa Charterhouse

itinerary

3

LUCCA AND ITS SURROUNDINGS

Poppi
Passo dei Mandrioli
Bibbiena
San Sepolcro
AREZZO
Castiglion Fiorentino
Cortona
Lago
M. Cetona 1148

LUCCA

- DUOMO
- MUSEUM OF THE OPERA DEL DUOMO
- GUINIGI TOWER
- ROMAN AMPHYTHEATRE
- VIA FILLUNGO
- PRAETORIAN PALACE
- CHURCH OF SAN MICHELE IN FORO
- CHURCH OF SAN FREDIANO
- PALAZZO DELLA PROVINCIA
- GIACOMO PUCCINI'S HOUSE
- PFANNER PALACE
- GUINIGI NATIONAL MUSEUM
- THE CITY WALLS

ITS SURROUNDINGS:

- BARGA
- CASTENUOVO GARFAGNANA
- PIETRASANTA
- VIAREGGIO
- FORTE DEI MARMI
- MASSACIUCCOLI
- GARFAGNANA
- BORGO A MOZZANO
- BAGNI DI LUCCA
- GROTTA DEL VENTO
- CAMAIORE
- VAL DI CASTELLO
- SERAVEZZA

LUCCA

According to some historians, the origins of the city of Lucca can be traced back to a Ligurian settlement; Lucca became a Roman colony in 180 B.C., as indicated by its streets, organised in a typical chessboard pattern.
In the IV century, under the rule of the Lombards, Lucca became the capital of the Marquisate of Tuscany.
Over the centuries it became an independent Commune, which enabled the city to protect its own trade interests, while also enjoying a period of great prosperity, despite Pisa contending control over the Tyrrhenian littoral.
During the first years of the XIV century, Lucca became a seigneurial district under several lords, such as Uguccione della Faggiola and Castruccio Castracani of the Antelminelli family, until, in 1369, it managed to gain its independence

and became a free republic governed by both the nobility and the bourgeoisie. Its republican government was only superseded by a seigneurial regime for a short period (1400-1430), during which Lucca was once again a Seigneury under the rule of Paolo Guinigi, a member of an important local family. The city's independence ended in 1805, when it was taken over by Napoleon, who turned it into a principality and put his sister Elisa Bonaparte, wife of Felice Baciocchi, in charge of it. In 1817, Lucca was under the rule of Maria Luigia Burbon-Parma. Her son, Carlo Ludovico, relinquished it to Leopold II, Grand Duke of Tuscany, in 1847.

On March 15, 1860, after a plebiscite, it finally joined the Kingdom of Italy.

DUOMO also known as SAN MARTINO Undoubtedly one of the most fascinating monuments in town, it was erected, legend has it, by St Frediano in the IV century and became the Bishop's seat in the VIII century. It was entirely rebuilt in 1060 for Bishop Anselm da Baggio, who was to become the future Pope Alexander II, and finished off at a later time, then entirely rebuilt at the beginning of the XIII century. Its asymmetrical facade, leaning against the bell tower, is in a superb Romanesque style: it features a ground-floor arcade and three ranges of open galleries above it. The upper section is by Guidetto da Como and dates back to 1204. The whole structure is covered with white, pink and green marble, with a superb decoration featuring bas-reliefs with the *Labors of the Months*: hunt scenes, peacocks and flowers. In the aisle and lintel at the left nave entrance there is the extraordinary *Deposition* by Nicola Pisano (circa 1860). Between the two arches, on the right, stands the statue of *St Martin and the Beggar*, a copy of the original statue, dating back to 1200 and displayed inside. On the right side of the facade stands the mighty bell tower, built in 1060 as a defensive tower. It underwent modifications in 1261, when transformed into an example of Lombard architecture and given single-lancet and quadruple-lancet windows at the time it was annexed to the cathedral. Its interior, restored between the end of 1300 and the beginning of 1400 in the gothic style, features a tripple nave in

Duomo, rear

the shape of a Latin cross. An elegant women's gallery overlooks the central nave. The cathedral houses several works of art, however, the most famous is undoubtedly the marble *Tomb of Ilaria del Carretto* by Jacopo della Quercia, dating back to 1408, situated in the left transept. Ilaria was the second wife of Paolo Guinigi; she died young in 1405. This is one of the most significant and moving sculptures of all times.

The central volume of the left nave houses the *Tempietto of the Holy Face*, an octagonal marble shrine by Matteo Civitali (1482-84) containing a wooden *Crucifix*, probably oriental in manufacture, dating back to the XI-XII century, featuring Christ clothed with a long garment. According to the medieval tradition, it was carved by Nicodemus, at the time of Jesus' Crucifixion.

On the left-side of the Cathedral, on Piazza degli Antelminelli, you will find the

MUSEUM OF THE OPERA DEL DUOMO It houses the Cathedral Treasure, made up of precious silver works, reliquaries and choir books.

From this square, on leaving the Cathedral, walk straight and you will reach via Sant'Anastasio (at the corner of via San Andrea), where you will see the bizarre

Jacopo della Quercia,
Tomb of Ilaria del Carretto

GUINIGI TOWER The tower is undoubtedly peculiar, crowned as it is with Holm oaks. It dates back to the second half of the XIV century and was built in brick; its bulk rests on a ground floor featuring arcades resting on stone pillars. The tower is part of a group of XIV-century palaces and towers, typical of Lucca Romanesque houses.

From via S. Andrea, turn right into via del Carmine, to reach the

ROMAN AMPHYTHEATRE Nothing is left of the ancient structure, but the original plan. The square outline is determined by the medieval buildings bordering the amphitheatre walls. Four arches lead to the square, perfectly aligned as they are to the four cardinal points and resting on the sites where the gates used by gladiators to enter the amphitheatre were. Studies proved evidence of the amphitheatre being built in the II century A.D.

Guinigi Tower
Piazza dell'Anfiteatro Romano

VIA FILLUNGO Once back into via San Andrea, walk down the road until you reach the crossroad with Via Fillungo, where you will find many shops with facades in an Art Nouveau style. This is the most famous street in town, where people go for walks or shopping. From here, turn right and walk down via Roma, leading to PIAZZA SAN MICHELE, the ancient forum of the Roman city.

At the corner with via Vittorio Veneto you will see the

PRAETORIAN PALACE Built of sandstone masonry and covered with a coat of plaster, it was begun in 1492, to the design of Matteo Civitali; in 1588, Vincenzo Civitali took charge of the works to enlarge it. It was the seat of both the Podestà and the Court. Nowadays it houses the offices of the Magistrate's Court.

CHURCH OF SAN MICHELE IN FORO Situated on the northeast side of the square, this is a Romanesque Church in the style of Pisa and Lucca. Back in the VIII century a church had been erected on this site, dedicated to St Michael. Around 1070, Pope Alexander II started its renovation, which was carried out up to the XIV century. By the transept right flank is the bell tower, the original battlements of which were replaced with new ones during the XIX century. Its apses is clearly in a Pisan style and almost surely by Diotisalvi. The interior features a triple-nave basilican ground-plan and houses several works of art.

Church of San Michele in Foro, a detail of its facade

CHURCH OF SAN FREDIANO (Piazza San Frediano) The excavations made underneath the current basilica confirmed it was built on a church of the VI century, probably built by St Frediano Bishop. The current church was erected between 1112 and 1147 and enlarged during the XIII century.

PALAZZO DELLA PROVINCIA previously known as PALAZZO DELLA SIGNORIA or DUCAL PALACE (Piazza Napoleone) This is the area hosting the Augustan Fortress, residence of Castruccio Castracani, destroyed to great acclaim in 1370. The current building is by Bartolomeo Ammannati (1578) and by Francesco Pini (1728), who completed the works.

Church of San Michele in Foro, lateral view

GIACOMO PUCCINI'S HOUSE (Via di Poggio) This is the house where the famous composer Giacomo Puccini (1858-1924) was born. It dates back to the XV century and accommodates the museum dedicated to the great Maestro.

PFANNER PALACE (previously Contrani Palace) This superb historical residence is open to the public. It was built in 1667 and its garden, designed in the XVIII century in a perfect Italian style, is considered to be among the most beautiful gardens of all Tuscany. Its interior houses a collection of court costumes of the XVIII and XIX centuries.

GUINIGI NATIONAL MUSEUM (Via della Quarconia) The villa built for Paolo Guinigi in 1418 accommodates the Museum displaying finds from the city churches and other archaeological finds from its surroundings.

THE CITY WALLS A nice visit to the city of Lucca would not be complete without the tour of the wall ring (stretching for 4.2 kilometers): it offers the visitor a very original walk on the fortified walls planted with trees and transformed into a park open to the public by Maria Luigia of the House of Bourbon, at the beginning of the XIX century.

These walls feature the third wall ring the city of Lucca had; built between 1504 and 1645, they survived almost unaltered throughout the centuries, except for the tree-lined paths and the insertion of other gates, that added to the three original ones.

A detail of the wall decoration

The walls, with their 12-metre external height and their 30-metre width at the base, were never used for military purposes, even though built to military standards and, therefore, equipped with 11 bulwarks, defended by 124 cannons and surrounded by a moat in places up to 30 metres deep.

Lucca is one of the rare medieval cities that still have beautiful intact walls.

City walls

THE SURROUNDINGS OF LUCCA

BARGA This is one of the most beautiful cities in the Serchio Valley, still retaining the distinctive feature of a Medieval town, as in 1341, when it asked Florence for protection, and always remained loyal to the city. It was in Barga that, in 1272, Barghesano di Bonaventura invented the spinning wheel for silk, for this fabric was already being produced on an industrial scale here. DUOMO Dedicated to San Cristoforo, it was built over several centuries, from the IX to the XX century. After the violent 1920 earthquake, it underwent massive reconstruction works. Its Romanesque facade features several sculptures depicting human forms, wild animals and tangled knots of artistic value. The most striking feature of its triple-nave interior is the superb marble pulpit in a typical Lucca style of the second half of the XII century. Besides this, also remarkable is a wooden sculpture from the XII century, depicting *St Christopher*, and the *Chapel of the Holy Sacrament*, with its prestigious Robbian works. Also worth seeing is the PRAETORIAN PALACE and the LOGGETTA DEL PODESTA', an example of XIV-century architecture, the XVI-century TOWN HALL, as well as the MARKET LOGGIA.

Barga, Duomo

Barga, Duomo, XII-century marble pulpit probably by Guido Bigarelli from Como

Pietrasanta, Duomo, Sergio Stagi, pulpit

CASTELNUOVO GARFAGNANA Surrounded by a suggestive mountain landscape, nowadays main town of the Garfagnana, Castelnuovo was long a Seigneury under the Este family. It was under the rule of Florence for a short period, at the beginning of the XVI century. Worth visiting is the ROCCA (Piazza Umberto I°). Started in the XII century, this fortress was later enlarged and entirely restored in 1946-48, due to severe damage suffered during World War II. The same happened to the XVI-century DUOMO, that was also rebuilt at the end of the 1940s. Ludovico Ariosto lived in Castelnuovo (1522-25), where he carried out the office of Commissary General of the Este family.

PIETRASANTA This is the biggest town in the Versilia hinterland. Named after its founder, Guiscardo Pietrasanta (1255), it was under the rule of several Seigneurs, until, in 1513, Pope Leo X granted the town to the Medici family, later replaced by the Lorraine family. It was the hometown of Eugenio Barsanti (1821-64), who invented the internal combustion engine. The town is famous today for its marble and onyx workmanship, and is home to much esteemed private art galleries. Worth visiting is the DUOMO, dedicated to San Martino. Erected between 1256-58, it was completed in 1330 and restored in 1630 and again in 1831. Its beautiful facade features three portals, with bas-reliefs in the style of the Pisan tradition, and a gothic rose window. Its triple-nave interior underwent modifications in the XVII century. It houses an interesting and richly sculptured marble-pulpit by Stagio Stagi (1504), an artist from Pietrasanta. Other works by the same artist are also housed in this cathedral. Worth mentioning are also artworks dating back to the XVII century. On the right side of the Cathedral rests the BAPTISTERY with its 1509 baptismal font, shaped like a cup. The BELL TOWER, built in brick masonry between the XV and the XVI centuries, also stands there, isolated, next to the Cathedral. Within the same square is the CHURCH OF SANT'AGOSTINO:

founded in the XIV century, it features a simple marble facade and a bell tower by its left side, dating back to 1780. Its cloister houses a cycle of XVI-century frescoes, dedicated to the homonym Saint. The PRAETORIAN PALACE, with its 1515 portal, and the clock tower known as TORRE DELLE ORE (1530-34) also overlook the Piazza del Duomo, along with the MONUMENT OF LEOPOLD II, famous for carrying out the first drainage works to defeat malaria in the Tuscan coast. Twin town of Pietrasanta is the coastal town of Marina di Pietrasanta, a pleasant seaside town, welcoming thousands of tourists each year.

Pietrasanta,
Monument of Leopold II

VIAREGGIO The town is renowned for its beautiful beaches, as well as for its Carnival, with its majestic and colourful papier-

Viareggio, seafront

mâché allegorical floats, attracting tourists from everywhere in the world each year. Many of the houses, hotels and clubs here are still in an Art Nouveau style, such as the famous Gran Caffè Margherita, designed by Galileo Chini.

The first nucleus of Viareggio was built in the first half of the XVI century, when the Republic of Lucca was left with only this stretch of coast. This is when its fortifications were built and the area improved. MATILDE TOWER, the most ancient building in town, was erected in 1541 to prevent barbarian incursions.

In the mid XIX century its port was restored, thereby promoting the development of maritime and fishing businesses.

The town became a seaside resort in 1861, when Giuseppe Barellai built some *seaside hostels*.

Burlamacco,
papier mâché art work,
symbol of Viareggio

Viareggio, *promenade*

Versilia with the Apuan Alps
in the background

MORE TO SEE IN THE SURROUNDINGS OF LUCCA

Not far from Lucca, Versilia is undoubtedly among the first places to visit. This is the name of the Tuscan coastline strip, with
its beaches stretching for about 30 kilometres, from Marina di
Carrara, in the North, to Torre del Lago, in the South.
This coast is scattered with lidos (beach facilities), hotels, vil-
las and tourist harbours, all surrounded by age-old pine-woods
that, along with the nearby Apuan Alps, grant a perfect climate.

Forte dei Marmi, the fortress

FORTE DEI MARMI This is the most famous seaside resort in the whole Versilia. It was named after the fortress, still
visible in the town centre, built for Grand Duke Pietro Leopoldo,
as a defence to the port and to the marble cargoes that arrived
here from the nearby Apuan Alps, ready to be shipped. With
its elegant clubs and exclusive discos, this is undoubtedly the
most lively town in Versilia.

Torre del Lago,
statue dedicated to
Giacomo Puccini

TORRE DEL LAGO PUCCINI
MASSACIUCCOLI From the tiny tourist resort of Torre del Lago, a road lined with linden
trees leads to the Lake of Massaciuccoli, where
you can visit the House of Giacomo Puccini.
Here the Maestro composed many of his works.
The villa is situated by the lake, a small expanse
of calm waters, where Puccini used to hunt water
fowls, his favourite hobby.
The villa still displays the musician's rifles, furniture
and heirlooms and, most importantly, it still houses the piano on which he composed his immortal
melodies. A hall, that has been transformed into a
chapel, houses Puccini and his wife's tombs.

Other places that are worth visiting are:

GARFAGNANA This big valley is surrounded by the Apuan
Alps at the West and by the Apennines at the North, acces-
sible from the towns of Barga, Serravezza and Castelnuovo
Garfagnana; it is an ideal place for sports in the open air like
canoeing or trekking. A must see here is, among others, the
ETHNOGRAPHIC MUSEUM OF SAN PELLEGRINO IN ALPE, in CAS-
TIGLIONE GARFAGNANA, and the PARCO DELL'ORECCHIELLA, ac-
commodating the Botanical Garden of Corfino.

Borgo a Mozzano

BORGO A MOZZANO (Devil's Bridge)

The town has a local economy based on agriculture. Its parish church houses many wooden statues of the XV-XVI centuries. Near the town of Borgo a Mozzano the PONTE DELLA MADD-ALENA crosses the river Serchio. It is also known as the DEVIL'S BRIDGE, a masterpiece of the XIII- or XIV-century architecture, featuring asymmetrical arcades.

Legend has it that the Devil offered to build the bridge upon being granted the soul of the first one to cross it; the local inhabitants, cleverer than the Devil himself, had him first build the bridge, then had a dog cross it.

BAGNI DI LUCCA
Famous spa resort, it has mild weather and very hot and radioactive waters, already renowned in the Middle Ages. In the mid XIX century, its Municipal Casino, built in 1840, was one of the most popular meeting-places for the nobility of Lucca and Europe altogether.

The largest and best known spa is that of Bagni Caldi, with water provided by the spring of *"Doccione"*; other spa resorts are Bagno San Giovanni and Bagno Bernabò.

Bagni di Lucca, the Serchio river

GROTTA DEL VENTO

Within the natural park of the Apuan Alps, founded in 1985, past the hermitage of Calomini, you will reach Fornovolasco, where you can visit its extremely suggestive Wind Grotto, a natural cave with underground galleries, discovered in 1964, rich in stalactites that add to its suggestive power.

CAMAIORE
Situated in the hinterland of Versilia, the town has a beautiful Collegiate Church, built in 1278, and a bell tower dating back to 1365, also housing some remarkable works of art. Twin town of Camaiore is Lido di Camaiore, on the coast.

VAL DI CASTELLO
The coast, stretching from La Spezia to Livorno and Val di Castello Carducci, offers a beautiful view. Along the main road of Val di Castello there is the house where Giosuè Carducci was born (1835-1907), today housing heirlooms and memories of the celebrated poet.

Camaiore, Collegiate Church

Seravezza

SERAVEZZA
This is an important site for marble extraction and takes its name from its location, at the junction of the Serra and Vezza rivers that, together, form the Versilia river. The Florentines have promoted the extraction of valuable marbles from this area since 1500. Michelangelo lived here in 1517, for he had an interest in the opening of the quarries on Mount Altissimo, the extraction site of the Statuario marble that the great artist used for creating many of his masterpieces.

itinerary

4

del
ione

ona

ia

Poppi Passo M. Fumaiolo
      dei Mandrioli 1407

Bibbiena

TINO

darno San Sepolcro

hi

AREZZO

Castiglion
Fiorentino

Cortona

Lago
Montepulciano

pulciano

M. Cetona
1148 ▲

adia S. Salvatore

dente

MASSA
- PIAZZA DEGLI ARANCI
- THE CATHEDRAL
- THE ROCCA

CARRARA
- DUOMO
- CIVIC MUSEUM OF MARBLE

THEIR SURROUNDINGS:
- THE QUARRIES
- FOSDINOVO
- SAN CARLO TERME

MASSA AND CARRARA

When, in 1473, the Marquis of Massa, Iacopo Malaspina, bought the Seigneury of Carrara from Count Antoniotto Filoremo from Genoa, the first nucleus of this town was finally erected. In modern history, the province of Massa and Carrara was established in 1859, when Garfagnana and Lunigiana became independent from the Duchy of Modena, in order to be annexed to the Kingdom of Italy.

The territory of Massa and Carrara boasts a purple heart for the contributions its people granted in the struggle against fascism during World War II. Characterised by a landscape dominated by the awesome Apuan Alps, the mountains from which the precious "white marble of Carrara" is extracted, the territory is also celebrated for its wonderful nature trails, as well as for its wine and food traditions.

Massa

Massa, Duomo, facade

Massa, Piazza degli Aranci

Carrara, Duomo, facade
below:
a detail of the marble rose
window

MASSA The town is located amidst the hills at the foot of the Apuan Alps; it has been famous since the X century as *curtis* of the Bishops of Luni. In the XI century, it became a fief under the rule of the Obertenghi family, who built the first fortified nucleus of the town. Contended over the centuries by Lucca, Pisa and Florence, it was granted, with Carrara,to the Malaspinas, Marquises of Fosdinovo (1442-1553), and later to the Cybo Malaspinas, lords of this territory until their last descendant married Ercole III d'Este, duke of Modena. In 1741, Massa and Carrara ended up under the dominion of the Duchy of Modena. In 1796, Massa was under the dominion of the French and, in 1806, it was granted in fief to Elisa Baciocchi and was annexed to Lucca. From 1815, the territory was back under the rule of the Este family, until 1859, when it was annexed to the Kingdom of Italy. During the aftermath of the last war, Massa became an industrial town and a tourist resort. The nearby hamlet of Marina, as a consequence of recent urban developments, has nowadays almost merged with the main town.

PIAZZA DEGLI ARANCI This square is in the heart of the old town, bordered on three sides by citrus trees. On its southern side rises the Cybo Malaspina Palace (today's Prefecture), once the residence of the town lords, restored by Alberico I Cybo Malaspina and by his descendents, thanks to whom the beautiful yard was built in 1665, to the design of Gian Francesco Bergamini.

THE CATHEDRAL (Basilica of San Pietro and San Francesco) It was originally a XIV-century church dedicated to San Remigio. It was enlarged for Giacomo Malaspina in 1447 and reworked several times, until it was given the actual shape in 1616. Its facade, in Carrara marble, dates back to 1936. Its interior houses the Burial Ground with the tombs of the Cybo-Malaspina family and some valuable works of ancient art that are worth seeing.

THE ROCCA also known as MALASPINA CASTLE It includes a medieval central nucleus, close to which the Malaspinas built their residence between the XV and the XVI centuries. The Renaissance palace is surrounded by bastions and, through an arcade, connected to the medieval structure.

CARRARA The town is renowned as the biggest Italian site for marble extraction, but also as one of the biggest worldwide. It was probably already famous two thousand years ago. The first settlements date back to the IX century B.C. and were erected by the Apuan Ligures, a people of Celtic origins. After the Romans conquered the territory in 180 B.C., its marble quarries started to be heavily exploited. After the fall of the Roman Empire, Carrara fell under the dominion of a number of rulers, until 1442, when it passed into the hands of the Malaspina Family; from then on it underwent the same political events as Massa.

DUOMO Its construction started in the XI century, and finished in the XIV century. The building is entirely covered with white and grey marble strips, as in the artistic style of Pisa and Lucca. Its triple-nave interior houses the remains of frescoes and several works of art, dated from the XIII to the XVI century. Its bell tower, erected in the mid XIII century, reproduces the style of Liguria.

CIVIC MUSEUM OF MARBLE This peculiar Museum offers the chance to learn and recognise the main methods to excavate, process and transport marble; it also displays the many types of marble that are extracted from the Apuan Alps, along with housing the Roman *shrine of Fantiscritti*, so-called for the small figures of the three depicted characters. Hercules, Jupiter and Dionysus are here depicted as "fanti", meaning "lads" in the local dialect.

Apuan Alps, Cava di Colonnata

THE SURROUNDINGS OF MASSA AND CARRARA

MARBLE QUARRIES 70% of Carrara marble comes from the quarries in the Apuan Alps, situated in the area known as Carrione, in the territory of Carrara. Here are the Canale di Colonnata, probably called such for the small hamlet of quarry workers ("cavatori") was originally a settlement of Roman slaves that had been brought here to extract marble, and the Canale dei Fantiscritti, named after the Roman bas-relief that was found here, still bearing the visible names of two famous visitors to the quarry: Giambologna (1598) and Canova (1800). Also here are the Canale di Torano, the Cave di Ravaccione, the Canale Bianco and the Canale Grande. Different types of marble are extracted from the quarries in the Apuan Alps; the most famous is the Statuario, the purest and most homogeneous, used by Michelangelo for his David. Other types include: Bianco Chiaro Ordinario, Bianco Porcellana, Bardiglio, Paonazzo, Fiordipesco, Cipollino, Breccia, Arabescato marble and many more. The marbles extracted in this area are exported worldwide.

FOSDINOVO It is a small town situated on a rock spur dominated, in its upper portion, by a castle bought in 1340 by the Malaspinas, who owned it until 1797. Damaged during the last war, it was later restored. The parish church of Fosdinovo houses the tomb of Galeotto Malaspina, who died in 1367, featuring the deceased as a lying figure on the lid.

Fosdinovo

SAN CARLO TERME This is a small thermal resort, with cold waters used in the treatment of gastroenteritis, hepatitis and renal diseases. The water is collected from the Aurelia spring. Water treatments are available from April to September.

Apuan Alps,
view of the Quarries

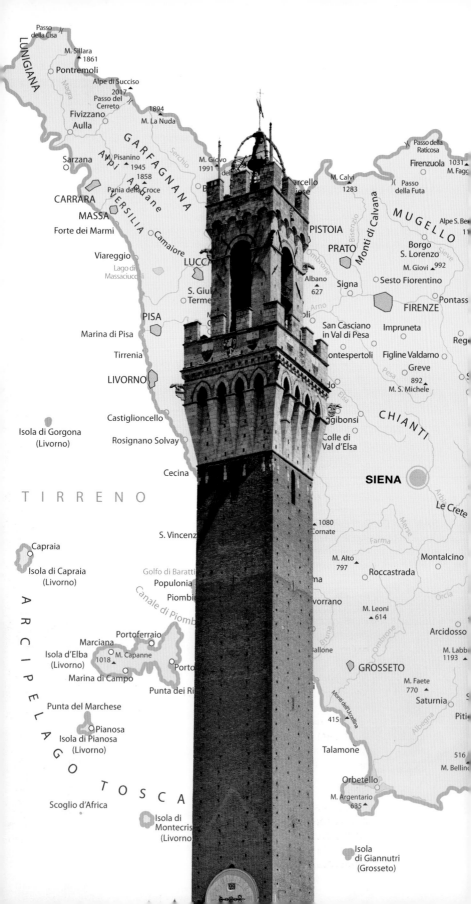

itinerary

del
one

na

a

oppi Passo
dei Mandrioli M. Fumaiolo
▲ 1407

Bibbiena

larno San Sepolcro ○

i

AREZZO

Castiglion
Fiorentino
○

Cortona ○

Lago
ontepulciano

ulciano

M. Cetona
1148 ▲

dia S. Salvatore

dente ○

SIENA
- PIAZZA DEL CAMPO
- TOWN HALL
- LOGGIA DELLA MERCANZIA
- DUOMO
- BAPTISTERY OF SAN GIOVANNI
- MUSEUM OF THE OPERA
- PALAZZO PICCOLOMINI
- NATIONAL ART GALLERY
- HOSPITAL OF SANTA MARIA DELLA SCALA
- HOUSE OF SANTA CATERINA
- PALAZZO CHIGI SARACINI
- CHURCH OF SAN DOMENICO
- MEDICEAN FORTRESS
- PALIO

ITS SURROUNDINGS:
- ABBEY OF MOUNT OLIVETO MAGGIORE
- ABBEY OF SAN GALGANO
- CHIANCIANO TERME
- COLLE VAL D'ELSA
- MONTALCINO
- MONTEPULCIANO
- PIENZA
- SAN GIMIGNANO
- ABBADIA SAN SALVATORE
- BUONCONVENTO
- CASTELNUOVO BERARDENGA
- CHARTERHOUSE OF PONTIGNANO
- SINALUNGA

SIENA AND ITS SURROUNDINGS

SIENA

The first document about Siena dates back to the year 70. The author, Tacito, depicts Siena as a Roman colony at the time of Emperor Augusto and calls it Saena Julia.

Siena rose to importance in the Middle Ages; the richest and most powerful citizens took control of the government and immediately rallied with the Ghibellines who were openly against the Guelphs of Florence. The power of Siena, which was the centre of the Tuscan Ghibellinism, came mostly from its merchants. They traded throughout Europe and even became financiers of the Pope. The rivalry with Florence started in the year 1141 and ended in 1235, when Florence imposed on Siena stringent peace accords. However, after a few years, the hostilities between the two cities resumed even more violent than before. On September 4th, 1260, the Florentine army was defeated at Montaperti (a small promontory located east of Siena).

After this victory, however, Siena's economy entered into crisis, in part due to a papal excommunication. The Ghibelline government, held by a Podestà and a Captain of the people, began to fade. After being defeated in 1269 by the Guelph troops of Carlo d'Angiò, in the plane between Colle Val d'Elsa and Monteriggioni, it was replaced by a Guelph government, ruled by the Council of the Thirty-six, which later became the Council of the Nine. It was during this time that the city was embellished with its most important monuments. Still, wars and famines continued, and the plague of 1348 killed a third of the population. Those events caused a general malaise that culminated in an uprising of the noble class that, helped by the lower middle class and by Emperor Charles IV, overthrew the government of the Nine. Following, there was a period of political instability, even though it was culturally dominated by two extraordinary figures: St Catherine from Siena (1347-1380) and St Bernardino (1380-1444), both preachers of peace.

From the XV to the XIX century Siena witnessed several
unstable governments, first the "Ten Priors' government",
then the "government of the Nobles ", then that of the "Nine".
Amongst them was Pandolfo Petrucci who, from 1487,
succeeded to form a government where all social classes
where represented.This administration was replaced by that
of the "Libertines", while imperial protection on the city grew,
and, in 1530, the troops of Charles V imposed a reorder of
the government that favoured the merchants. In 1552, the
rebels, who had allied with France and with the escaped
Florentines headed by Piero Strozzi, succeeded in throwing
out the imperialists. However, this fight was useless: on April
17, 1555, following a siege the Sieneses heroically countered
with their offensive for about two years, an army of Germans,
Spanish and Italians, with Gian Giacomo de'Medici in
command, finally inflicted a crushing defeat to the weakened
town and laid siege to it. This is how Siena was eventually
annexed to the Grand Duchy of Tuscany, for the glory of
Cosimo I. Later, just like Tuscany, the town passed under the
dominion of the House of Lorraine. At the time of Napoleon's
rule, it became the capital of the Department of Ombrone.
Once back under the rule of the House of Lorraine, after
Napoleon's defeat, Siena was the first town in Tuscany to
choose to be annexed to the Kingdom of Italy, in 1859.

PIAZZA DEL CAMPO also known as CAMPO This square, the core of the administrative activities of Siena, is situated on the ridges of the three hills, on top of which the town was erected. It is among one of the most ancient and beautiful squares worldwide. Shaped like a shell in the XII century, it was paved with brick laid edge in 1347 and consists of nine sectors with stone stripes separating them, a reminder of the Government of the Nine, under the rule of which both the square and the Palazzo Pubblico were

Piazza del Campo

built. All around the brick pavement unfolds a ring-track, where the famous Palio horse race is run. In the middle of the hemicycle is situated the superb Fonte Gaia (a copy of the original, dating back to last century) by Jacopo della Quercia, built between 1409 and 1419 and alimented by a 1344 aqueduct, stretching for 25 km.

THE TOWN HALL Opposite the fountain, as if the whole convex square would radiate from it, rises the elegant Palazzo Pubblico: one of the most beautiful gothic palaces in Tuscany. Built to be the seat of the Sienese government, it housed the Seigneury and the Podestà and is, at present, the seat of the local government offices. Built in stone and brickwork from 1297 to 1310, it was extended from its right flank in 1327, when the jails were added. Later, from 1330 to 1342, it underwent a new extension, meant to create the Hall of the Great Council. Its superb facade features a central three-storey volume and two lateral two-storey volumes. On its left side stands out the elegant Torre del Mangia, named after its first bell ringer, Giovanni di Duccio, known as Mangia-guadagni or else, as Mangia. The tower (102 m. tall up to the top of its lightning conductor) was built by the brothers Minuccio and Francesco di Rinaldo, between 1338 and 1348, in Cotto tiles, with a stone bell tower built to the design of Lippo Menni (1341). 505 steps lead to the top. At the base of the tower there is the Cappella di Piazza, a marble loggia built to fulfil a vow by those who survived the black death killing many in 1348. It was designed by Domenico di Agostino in 1352. Antonio Federighi modified it according to the Renaissance taste between 1463 and 1468.

It accommodates the CIVIC MUSEUM, with its Hall of the Globe

Town Hall

situated on the first floor (the hall once housed a rolling map that was lost, painted by Ambrogio Lorenzetti). Its left wall features the magnificent fresco of the *Majesty* by Simone Martini (1315), one of the most beautiful frescoes of Siena XIV-century production. Its left wall features the magnificent fresco of the *Majesty* by Simone Martini (1315), one of the most beautiful frescoes of Siena fourteenth-century production. Its right wall features instead the *Guidoriccio da Fogliano*, always by Simone Martini (1328), that is perhaps the most famous fresco of Siena Gothic production; the *Hall of Peace*, seat of the Seigneurs, features the greatest cycle of the medieval pagan paintings, depicting scenes from contemporary life. The *Hall of the Nine* features the frescoes depicting the *Allegories of the good and the bad government both in town and in the country-side*, painted by Ambrogio Lorenzetti between 1338 and 1340. The Civic Museum also includes other halls, with frescoes painted between the XIV and the XV centuries, exception made for the *Hall of the Risorgimento*, frescoed during the XIX century.

LOGGIA DELLA MERCANZIA Behind Piazza del Campo rises the superb Loggia della Mercanzia, also known as the Merchants' loggia or St Paul's Loggia. It was built between 1417 and 1444. Here bankers and merchants used to gather to make business deals.

Loggia della Mercanzia

Walking through the streets of Siena, dominated by wonderful XIV-century buildings, you will reach Piazza del Duomo.

DUOMO Dedicated to the Madonna Assunta (Our Lady of Assumption), it was built in a pure Gothic style. It is one of the most beautiful medieval churches in Italy. It was erected on the ruins of an ancient, pre-existing church in the mid XII century. In 1196, the masons' guild of the Works of Santa Maria's was charged with completing it. In 1215, the essential nucleus had been completed and, between 1259 and 1264, also its hexagonal dome had been built. In 1339, a second massive addition was planned, foreseeing the erection of a new nave on the south flank of the existing church, so as to transform the existing structure into the transept of the new Cathedral. All had to be done under the direction of Lando di Pietro. However, due to a number of reasons, among which some basic errors in the statistical calculations, not to mention the huge costs that a devastated town, also decimated by the 1348 black death, would have had to bear, the project was abandoned. Therefore, the precarious sections were demolished and works were resumed to simply complete the existing church.

Duomo

Its beautiful FACADE in white marble, also featuring Siena-red and Prato-green marbles, was mainly decorated with sculptures. The lower section, in a Romanesque style with gothic influences, is by Giovanni Pisano (1284-96), whereas the upper section, in a late Gothic style, was built between 1382 and 1390. Almost all the statues on view are copies of the originals kept in the Museum of the Opera. It houses XIX-century mosaics and features a Romanesque bell tower.

Duomo,
Michelangelo Buonarroti,
Piccolomini Altar

Its INTERIOR features a triple-nave, Latin-cross structure with some architectural irregularities, due to the long construction period. The cathedral is a display of works of art among which the marble mosaic floor stands out. It consists of 56 panels, which saw more than forty artists at work from the XV to the XIX century. All panels are inlaid (done on wood, marble or hard stones, inlaid work or inlay is how the finished product is referred to) and in graffito work (widely used during the Renaissance, graffito is obtained by inscribing a light-coloured layer that rests on a darker layer) in white and black marbles, sometimes in polychrome marbles. The pulpit by Nicola Pisano (1266-68), helped by his son Giovanni and by Arnolfo di Cambio, is in white marble and features an octagonal plan. It is one of the most beautiful works of the Italian Gothic tradition. The Chapel of San Giovanni Battista by Giovanni di Stefano (1482) is an elegant Renaissance Chapel. The Piccolomini Library was founded in 1495 by Francesco Todeschini Piccolomini (later Pope Pius III), in order to store the collection owned by his uncle, Pope Pius II (Enea Silvio Piccolomini). It is decorated with frescoes by Pinturicchio (1502-09), with *scenes from the life of Pius II*.

BAPTISTERY OF SAN GIOVANNI It was built between 1316 and 1325, underneath the eastern bays of the Cathedral Choir, to the design of Camaino di Crescentino. Its triple-nave interior houses a valuable baptismal font by the great artists of the time: among these are Donatello (a bronze relief with *Herod's banquet* and the statues of *Faith* and *Hope*), Lorenzo Ghiberti, Jacopo della Quercia and others.

Museum of the Opera
Duccio di Buoninsegna,
Madonna on the Throne

Palazzo Piccolomini

MUSEUM OF THE OPERA It is situated in the lateral, unfinished nave, part of which had to be the new Duomo. If was founded in 1870, mainly to house works from the Duomo, signed, among others, by Duccio di Buoninsegna, Giovanni Pisano, Simone Martini, Jacopo della Quercia, Pietro Lorenzetti. Famous is the *Majesty* by Duccio di Buoninsegna (1308-11), that remained on the main altar until 1505: it is the first masterpiece of all Sienese painting production.

PALAZZO PICCOLOMINI (Via Banchi di Sotto) It is a Florentine Renaissance building, started in 1469 by Pietro Paolo Porrina, to the design of Bernardo Rossellino. Built for the Piccolomini family, it was the most important private palace in Siena. It nowadays hosts the State Archives.

NATIONAL ART GALLERY (Via San Pietro) Accommodated in the Brigidi and in the Buonsignori Palaces (mighty late-gothic buildings, erected during the first half of the XV century), it houses the most important paintings of the Sienese school from the XIII to the XVIII century. Worth seeing is the *City by the Sea* by Lorenzetti – a unique example in all European painting tradition preceding the XVI century, only depicting a landscape – the *Madonna with Child*, also by Ambrogio Lorenzetti and the magnificent *Altarpiece for the Carmelite Church* by Pietro Lorenzetti.

HOSPITAL OF SANTA MARIA DELLA SCALA Situated opposite the Cathedral, it is one of the most ancient hospitals in Europe.

It was turned into a museum in the last few years. This huge complex (350,000 cubic metres), that has preserved undamaged the testimonies of one thousand years of the town history, houses works of great artists and is a superb synthesis of the town culture.

HOUSE OF SANTA CATERINA
(Costa di Sant'Antonio) This is the house where Caterina Benincasa (1347-80) was born. At the age of eight she took her vows and saw visions many times; during one of these visions she received the stigmata. She died in Rome and was canonized in 1461 and is the Patron Saint of Siena and Italy.

PALAZZO CHIGI - SARACINI (Via di Città) Started in the XII century and built in stone and brick masonry, it features a cut-off stone tower. It accommodates the famous Accademia Musicale Chigiana, founded in 1932 by Count Guido Chigi-Saracini.

CHURCH OF SAN DOMENICO Entirely built in brick masonry, according to a gothic-Cistercian style, it was started in 1226 and completed in 1465. The tower, however, dates back to 1340. The church interior features an Egyptian cross and a single nave. The Chapel of S. Caterina, with frescoes by Sodoma (1526), houses the head of the Saint. It was here that Caterina received the stigmata. The Chapel of the Vaults houses the portrait of the Saint by Andrea Vanni, her contemporary, dating back to 1380.

Palazzo Chigi-Saracini

MEDICEAN FORTRESS also known as FORTE DI SANTA BARBARA (Viale Maccari) It was erected for Cosimo I, in 1560, to the design of Baldassarre Lanci. In 1937 its bastions were opened to the public. It nowadays also accommodates an open-air theatre.

Church of San Domenico

PALIO This horse race is run each year in Piazza del Campo, first on July 2, as established in the first half of the XVII century, to celebrate a miracle by the Virgin Mary of Provenzano, and on August 16, to celebrate the Assunta (Assumption of the Virgin Mary in Heaven, as of the catholic dogma), as established in 1147. The Palio consists of a parade (a historical pageant) of the contradas

Palio

and of a horse race, with jockeys riding bareback. Nowadays there are 17 contradas: *Aquila, Chiocciola, Onda, Pantera, Selva, Tartuca, Civetta, Leocorno, Nicchio, Torre, Valdimontone, Bruco, Drago, Giraffa, Istrice, Lupa, Oca.* Among these, ten contradas, in turn, compete riding on horses selected and allocated by lot, that have been blessed beforehand, in the churches of the contradas. The actual race lasts no longer than one and a half minutes, during which the supporters of the various contradas crowd the square, thus eliciting an utmost tense atmosphere, rich in rivalry. The winning contrada is awarded a Palio (commonly referred to as *Cencio* – a painted cloth) or Standard; the night of the victory the winning district is all lit up and feasting.

THE SURROUNDINGS OF SIENA

ABBEY OF MOUNT OLIVETO MAGGIORE A panoramic road, bordered in places by a forest of cypresses and offering one of the most fascinating views of Tuscany, leads to the solitary Abbey of Mount Oliveto Maggiore, situated on a woody hill, dominating the "Crete Senesi". The big monastery was founded in 1313 by Bernardo Tolomei (1272-1348), a well educated man from a rich and famous Sienese family, who, at some point in his life, abandoned everything to follow the rule of St Benedict. Bernardo retired in this place, owned by his family, with the approval of the Bishop of Arezzo (Guido Tarlati) and, from 1344, also with the consent of Pope Clement VI, who confirmed the Congregation of Mount Oliveto. Between the XV and the XVI century, the monastery was one of the main cultural and artistic centres of the Catholic world and is still nowadays the residence of the Abbot General of the Benedictine Congregation of Mount Oliveto. The monastery is accessible from a medieval palace (1393), erected as a defence to the monastic complex, decorated with terracottas in the style of Della Robbia. Past this palace, the courtyard opens

Abbey of Mount Oliveto
Maggiore

onto an avenue that, past the botanical garden and a fish pond (1533), leads to the CHURCH, built between 1400 and 1417 and decorated with an elegant portal. Its one-nave interior, redecorated in a Baroque style in 1772, features very beautiful wooden choir stalls, carved and inlaid by Friar Giovanni da Verona (1503-1505). In the middle of the dome stands out *Our Lady of Assumption* by Jacopo Ligozzi and, also by him, the *Nativity of the Virgin Mary* (1598), situated behind the main altar. Flanking the church is the GREAT CLOISTER, featuring a rectangular plan, built between 1427 and 1474, decorated with frescoes by Luca Signorelli and Sodoma, that make one of the most valuable pictorial cycles of Italian Renaissance. The stories depict the *Life of St Benedict* and were completed at two different times: Signorelli was the first to work at them from 1497 to 1498, followed by Sodoma from 1505 to 1508. The cycle unfolds from the eastern wall, perfectly merging with the architecture of the place. From the GREAT CLOISTER, through the MIDDLE CLOISTER you will access the REFECTORY, decorated by Friar Paolo Novelli (1670).

The first floor of the monastery features the LIBRARY HALL, built in 1518; the MONASTIC LIBRARY, housing 40,000 books; the PHARMACY, housing a collection of XVII century vases, and the CHAPTER HALL, referred to as Definitorio, built in 1540.

Abbey of San Galgano

ABBEY OF SAN GALGANO This decaying and solitary building rises in the silence of a thick wood, in contrast with the proud somptuousness of this structure, that exalts its dramatic beauty. Built by the Cistercians monks between 1224 and 1288, it contributed to spreading the gothic architectural structures of the transalpine Churches in Tuscany. After it had grown into a centre of power, despite the monks preaching about poverty, the abbey held estates in the region of Siena and Grosseto and its monks became famous doctors, judges, notaries and architects.

However, bad management resulted in a rapid decline of the abbey. Repeated pillages at the end of the XIV century, perpetrated by Commander Giovanni Acuto, in 1397, resulted in an inexorable collapse of the abbey between the XV and the XVI century that, by then, was only inhabited by its Abbot. With the suppression of all religious orders, a lot of the premises remained empty and started to deteriorate. In 1722, huge cracks appeared in its walls, in 1786 the bell tower collapsed and, shortly after, also the roof crumbled down. The abbey interior, entirely covered in grass, is probably the most suggestive thing to see. The triple-nave abbey has the sky for roof. On the right side of the church, the MONASTERY still features a well preserved CHAPTER HALL, the MONKS' HALL and the CLOISTER, with the monks' cells on the upper floor. Close to the Abbey, on Mount Siepi, lies the SMALL CHURCH OF SAN GALGANO; built in a Sienese Romanesque style, it features a circular plan with concentric rings of Cotto tiles and bricks. Next to it lies a chapel, built at the beginning of the XIV century, frescoed in

Abbey of San Galgano, interior

1344 by Ambrogio Lorenzetti with *Scenes from the life of San Galgano*. Galgano Guidotti was a knight from a noble family of Chiusdino. Born in 1148, he led a brave but dissolute life, until he became close to God and renounced the world. He also tried to break his sword on a rock, to repudiate the horrors of war. The sword, however, got stuck into the rock, only showing its hilt, to form a cross.

Galgano interpreted this as a sign from God and retired to live as a hermit on Mount Siepi, where the small church was erected. He died here in 1181 and was canonized by Pope Urban III, in 1185. The "sword in the rock" is still visible (though it is a modern copy) in the middle of the small church dedicated to San Galgano.

CHIANCIANO TERME

CHIANCIANO TERME Situated in the Southern Valdichiana, this is one of the most celebrated thermal resorts in Italy, specialised in the treatment of liver diseases.

Chianciano is divided into the new town, with its big and modern hotels, thermal gardens, pools, but also private houses and avenues scattered with beautiful shops, and an old town, Chianciano Vecchia, probably of Etruscan origins, still featuring the ruins of its medieval walls. The thermal waters of Chianciano were already resorted to by the Etruscans and the Romans, but were also pretty much appreciated during the Middle Ages and the Medicean period. It was however in 1915 that Chianciano's fame spread, due to the founding of the "Società delle Terme di Chianciano", providing the area with an adequate hydraulic system and taking care of bottling its waters. Over the years, the town has developed increasingly, due to the building of the big spa resorts and the opening of an Institute for Biological and Chemical Research.

Abbey of San Galgano, interior

Four water springs are used today: ACQUA DI SILLENE, ACQUA DI FUCOLI, ACQUA SANTA AND ACQUA DI SANTA ELENA, channelled into fountains and pools. They are also used to produce the famous mud, made of clay macerated into water.

Chianciano Terme

COLLE VAL D'ELSA The town rises on the left bank of the river Elsa and is divided into the Piano, that is the modern town, with shops selling local crystal ware, and Colle Alta, rich in medieval palaces and monuments. It was under the rule of the Bishops of Volterra for ten centuries, then became a free commune in the XII century. From 1333 the town passed under the rule of Florence that had long contended it to Siena. Between the XI and the XII century wool factories largely developed in this area, along with paper factories and, from the mid XIV century, crystal-ware factories, turning Colle Val d'Elsa into one of the most important production centres. All these activities were made possible by a still existing pipeline system, the Gore, taking its motive power from the water of the river Elsa.

This was the hometown of Arnolfo di Cambio (approximately 1245-1302), an ingenious architect and sculptor. Colle Alta is still partially surrounded by its XII century walls.

Church of Santa Maria in Canonica

PALAZZO CAMPANA This is a peculiar palace, built in 1539 to the design of Giuliano di Baccio d'Agnolo. Its central portal features an entrance arch to the CASTLE, a built-up-area characterised by small medieval and stately houses of the Renaissance period.

PRAETORIAN PALACE (Piazza del Duomo) It was built in 1335 and was partially altered by restoration interventions. It accommodates the ARCHAEOLOGICAL MUSEUM or *Antiquarium*, housing Etruscans finds from the Val d'Elsa, dating back to a period ranging from the IV to the I century B.C.

DUOMO (Piazza del Duomo) Built between 1603 and 1619 on a pre-existing Roman parish church, the Cathedral features a rear facade, compared to the bell tower, built in 1815. Its interior features a triple-nave structure, housing some artworks, among which is the beautiful bronze lectern by Pietro Tacca.

PALAZZO VESCOVILE (Via del Castello) The Bishop's Palace accommodates a small Museum of Sacred Art, displaying valuable vestments and furniture.

Tower-House of Arnolfo di Cambio

Borgo di Santa Caterina, Donjon and Porta Nuova

PALAZZO DEI PRIORI (Via del Castello) Its beautiful facade decorated with graffito works, features cherubs and the Medicean coat of arms. It accommodates the CIVIC MUSEUM, collecting artworks, mainly paintings, from the Renaissance period.

CHURCH OF SANTA MARIA IN CANONICA (Via del Castello) Built in a Romanesque-Pisan style in the XII century, it was re-worked in the XVIII century and restored in the XX century. Its interior houses a beautiful tabernacle, the *Madonna on the Throne and Saints*, probably by Pier Francesco Fiorentino, dating back to the second half of the XV century.

TOWER-HOUSE OF ARNOLFO DI CAMBIO (Via del Castello) It was the birthplace of Arnolfo di Cambio. He was a great artist, who worked mainly in Florence (the tower of Palazzo Vecchio is by him). Its tower is a typical example of XIII-century architecture.

PORTA NOVA also known as PORTA SALIS (Via Gracco del Secco) A typical Renaissance building, it was erected to military standards in the XV-XVI centuries, featuring two defensive, cylindrical towers, probably designed by Giuliano da Sangallo.

MONTALCINO

MONTALCINO It is one of the most fascinating Tuscan towns, famous for its local wine, the celebrated Brunello, available in the wine bars scattered along the steep narrow roads, flanked by Sienese late-medieval buildings. Montalcino was a free commune, contended by Florence and Siena, which eventually subjugated it in 1260. After the battle of Montaperti, the town managed to defy the troops of Clement VII (1525), as well as the imperial troops (1553), but was eventually defeated and had to submit to Cosimo I de'Medici. From then onwards, the town's history became one with that of the Grand Duchy of Tuscany.

Montalcino

THE TOWN HALL (Costa del Municipio) Previously known as Palazzo dei Priori, it was built between the XIII and the XIV century and features a tall tower in stone and brick masonry.

CHURCH OF SAN EGIDIO Built in 1325, the Church features an interior that was altered in the XVII century.

CHURCH OF SAN AGOSTINO It was built in the XIV century in a Romanesque-gothic style.

CIVIC, DIOCESAN AND ARCHAEOLOGICAL REUNITED MUSEUMS (Via Ricasoli) Accommodated in a building adjacent to the Church of St Augustine, a former monastery, the Reunited Museums house interesting artworks, among which is a Byzantine *Crucifix* of the XIII century and a *Madonna with Child and St Catherine* by Domenico Beccafumi. The collection also includes *St Peter and St Paul* by Ambrogio Lorenzetti and a *Madonna with Child* by Simone Martini.

Montalcino Brunello wine

DUOMO (SAN SALVATORE) The Cathedral was built between 1818 and 1832 in a Neo Classical style, to the design of Agostino Fantastici. It was erected on a pre-existing Romanesque parish church. Its interior houses two important paintings by Francesco Vanni: the *Immaculate Conception and St John the Baptist*.

ROCCA or FORTRESS It is situated on the highest spot of the town. Built for the Sieneses, in 1361, it was meant to be a military bastion. It is an important example of military architecture, planned by Mino Foresi and Domenico di Feo, who used a portion of the ancient XIII-century walls.
Its mighty bastions were added in 1571 for Cosimo I and, in 1599, the external spur was added. It is open to the public and actually features very suggestive premises, among which a wine cellar for tasting the Brunello wine. One of the rooms houses a Sienese standard, a reminder of the hospitality granted to a group of rebels after Florence had conquered Siena.

Montalcino,
Abbey of Sant'Antimo

Montalcino, Rocca

Montepulciano

MONTEPULCIANO The town is situated on a crest between the Valdichiana and the Val d'Orcia, and is still surrounded by the walls designed in 1511 by Antonio da Sangallo the Young. It still preserves superb buildings in a Florentine late-Renaissance style. A walk in Montepulciano will lead you through suggestive alleys, mainly steep and narrow, dating back to the Middle Ages, when the Etruscan town was contended between Siena and Florence. It eventually and permanently fell under the dominion of Florence, to which it remained loyal even during the Medicean period, thus merging its history with that of the Grand Duchy of Tuscany. Agnolo Ambrogini (1454-94), and Cardinal Roberto Bellarmino (1532-1621) were born here. The first, known as Poliziano, was one of the greatest poets of all Italian Renaissance; the second, a Jesuit father and theoretician of the Counter-reform, is still known for impeaching Galileo Galilei. The wonderful countryside surrounding Montepulciano produces the renowned "noble wine of Montepulciano", available in any of the wine bars opened in the typical shops and wine cellars.

DUOMO (Piazza Grande) It was built on the ruins of an ancient parish church, between 1592 and 1630, to the plan of Ippolito Scalza. It features a simple and rough facade that was left unfinished, pretty much in contrast with its triple-nave interior, housing several works of art, among which, on the main altar, a superb triptych depicting the *Assumption* by the Sienese Taddeo di Bartolo, dating back to 1401. Only the bell tower remains of the ancient parish church.

Town Hall

THE TOWN HALL (Piazza Grande) Michelozzo, a famous Florentine architect, was charged with transforming the pre-existing medieval building in 1440. The building is a smaller copy of Palazzo Vecchio in Florence. It offers a superb view, ranging from the Trasimeno Lake to Mount Amiata and beyond, to include Siena.

PALAZZO TARUGI Piazza Grande) This is a beautiful example of mannerist architecture by Vignola, according to some, though most probably by Antonio da Sangallo the Old. It was erected on a mighty arcade.

PALACE OF THE PEOPLE'S CAPTAIN (Piazza Grande) This XIV-century building nowadays accommodates the magistrate's court. Opposite the palace stands the Well of the Griffons and Lions (1520), one of the most beautiful wells in Italy.

Palazzo Tarugi,
a detail of Piazza Grande

PALAZZO NERI ORSELLI (Via Ricci) Built in a Sienese Gothic style, it nowadays accommodates the Civic Museum, housing some beautiful glazed terracottas by Andrea della Robbia, along with a number of paintings (XVI - XVIII centuries).

CHURCH OF SANT'AGOSTINO (Piazza Michelozzo) Founded in 1285, the Church was entirely renovated in 1429. Its travertine facade was probably made in collaboration with Michelozzo. Surely enough, the wonderful portal with a terracotta lunette depicting the *Madonna with Child and Saints John the Baptist and Augustine* is by Michelozzo. The one-nave interior was reworked at the end of the XVIII century, when its original structure was altered.

POLIZIANO'S HOUSE (Via Poliziano) This is a XIV- or XV-century building that was reworked several times, featuring a plaque commemorating the birth of the great poet. Also worth visiting is the PALAZZO AVIGNONESI (Via Roma), designed by Vignola to late-Renaissance standards, the MARKET LOGGIA (Via Roma), designed by Ippolito Scalza at the end of the XVI century, and PALAZZO CERVINI (Via Cavour), commissioned to Sangallo by Cardinal Marcello Cervini, later to become Pope Marcellus II.

CHURCH OF SAN BIAGIO It is a masterpiece by Antonio da Sangallo the Old, who, between 1518 and 1545, built one of the masterpieces of the Tuscan Cinquecento here. The church features a Greek cross plan and is built in travertine, that has turned golden brown with time, which makes it even more beautiful than it was. The church rises as a solitary structure, in the middle of the grassland, which intensifies its magnificence.

Montepulciano,
Church of San Biagio

Its facade is flanked by two bell towers, one of which was left unfinished, due to Sangallo's death. Its interior, with a slightly altered presbytery, due to Baroque stuccoes and gildings, inspires a calm solemnity. The main altar houses the mighty marble altar frontal made by Giannozzo and Lisandro Albertini in 1584. On the left side of the church is the Rectory, a posthumous structure, built in 1595, once again to the design of Sangallo, just like the well opposite the rectory.

PIENZA Wonderful town situated on top of a hill, it offers a marvellous view of the surrounding landscapes. It was named such by Pope Enea Silvio Piccolomini, eminent scholar, politician and poet, who was born here in 1405, when the small hamlet was still called Corsignano.

When he was appointed Pope, in 1458, Piccolomini took up the name of Pius II and was almost immediately struck by the idea of transforming his hometown into a small city. Therefore, he charged Bernardo Rossellino with carrying out this project. In three years, the latter nearly accomplished this transformation, and turned the town into a small Renaissance town, almost an "ideal town", built to the standards of the contemporary humanistic culture.

Pienza (the name of which was established with a Papal Bill in 1462), besides being an almost unique example of town planning, is one of the most famous towns in Italy, for the production of "pecorino" cheese, to be bought in any of the many characteristic shops you will find along its pleasant roads. The most important buildings in Pienza are concentrated in the main square: PIAZZA PIO II, a real treasure chest housing gems like the WELL, designed by Rossellino in 1462, the CATHEDRAL, dedicated to the Virgin Mary of Assumption, the TOWN HALL and PALAZZO PICCOLOMINI.

Pienza

Pienza, a store selling
typical products

Pienza, Duomo

CATHEDRAL Built to the design of Rossellino (1459-92), according to Renaissance standards as in the style of Leon Battista Alberti, the Cathedral features a travertine facade, surmounted by the coat of arms of Pope Pius II, and a bright triple-nave interior housing several works of art, most of which were made between 1461 and 1463, to decorate the Cathedral. Unfortunately, a subsidence of the soil in the eastern side of the church caused cracks in the walls and a split on the floor only a few years after its completion. The structure is continuously undergoing reinforcement interventions that, however, could not stop the subsidence phenomenon so far. On the left side of the Cathedral rests the CANONS' HOUSE, a Renaissance building, seat of the CATHEDRAL MUSEUM, founded in 1901 to store the artworks that were removed from the church. Next to this building is the BISHOP'S PALACE, previously known as Palazzo Borgia, restored in a Renaissance style for the future Pope Alexander VI, at the time he was still Cardinal Rodrigo Borgia. Opposite the Cathedral is the TOWN HALL, built in travertine and largely restored in 1900.

PALAZZO PICCOLOMINI On the right side of the Cathedral stands the mighty Piccolomini Palace, designed by Rossellino (1459-62), who took inspiration from the Rucellai Palace in Florence, designed by Leon Battista Alberti. The palace, in rustic work, features three storeys with equally spaced double-lancet windows and pilaster strips; the left side of the yard, featuring elegant arcades resting on columns with Corinthian capitals, opens onto a roof garden, with a vaulted gallery and arches overlooking it from the first floor. The palace, residence of the Piccolomini family until 1968, is partially open to the public and still houses furniture, paintings, books and other valuable objects.

Pienza, Town Hall

PALAZZO AMMANNATI (Corso Rossellino) This solemn XV-century building was erected for Cardinal Giacomo Ammannati, a friend of Pius II's.

CHURCH OF SAN FRANCESCO (Corso Rossellino) Built at the end of the XIII century, in a very simple style, the Church features a single-nave interior, and houses fragments of frescoes dating back to the XIV and the XV centuries.

San Gimignano,
Piazza della Cisterna

SAN GIMIGNANO Inhabited since Etruscan times, the town became a free Commune in the XII century. Later it sided with the Guelphs and Florence until, in 1354, it permanently submitted to the *city of the lily*. Urban development in San Giminiano is due to the fact that the town rests on the ancient Via Francigena (one of the main Medieval roads for pilgrims connecting Rome to Northern Europe, and therefore connecting with the most important pilgrimage routes), along which the biggest towers and tower-houses of the XII and the XIII century were built, that belonged to the most important families (only 15 of the 72 towers that were erected still exist).

The ancient town started to decline at the beginning of the XIV century. However, luckily enough, its original structure was left unaltered, thus enabling us to appreciate the Tuscan medieval urban-planning strategies. The heart of the town is PIAZZA DEL DUOMO, dominated by the most important buildings in San Giminiano.

COLLEGIATE CHURCH or DUOMO OF SANTA MARIA ASSUNTA Consecrated in 1148, the Church was enlarged by Giuliano da Maiano, in 1460. Its triple-nave interior is richly decorated with a large cycle of frescoes, the most important of which are: the *New Testament* in the right nave, by Barna da Siena (second half of the XIV century) and the *Old Testament* by Bartolo di Fredi (circa 1367) in the left nave. Its internal facade is frescoed with the *Last Judgement* by Taddeo di Bartolo (1393-96). Moreover, the middle nave features the CHAPEL OF SANTA FINA, designed by Giuliano and Benedetto da Maiano and frescoed by Ghirlandaio in 1475, with scenes from Saint Fina's life.

San Gimignano,
Palazzo Vecchio del Podestà

PALAZZO DEL PODESTÀ Already rebuilt in 1239, it was extended in 1337. Its ground floor features a large vault or loggia, providing access to the palace, and a tower, known as the *Rognosa* (51 m. of height), that had to be, by law, the highest tower in San Giminiano.

PALAZZO DEL POPOLO or NEW PALACE OF THE PODESTÀ It is nowadays the seat of the local government. It was built in 1288 and enlarged in 1323. It also accommodates the CIVIC MUSEUM, displaying the imposing *Majesty* by Lippo Memmi (signed and dated 1317), inspired to that by Simone Martini, besides a wonderful collection of paintings dated XIII and XVI century.

PIAZZA DELLA CISTERNA The square, once destined to host the market, feasts and tournaments, was named after a cistern dated 1287, around which a number of houses and medieval towers were erected.

MUSEUM OF SACRED ART The museum is located in the ancient Chaplains' Dormitory, and displays a collection of valuable objects and artworks removed from the Duomo and from the churches scattered in the territory of San Giminiano.

ROCCA DI MONTESTAFFOLI Built in 1353, the fortress was almost entirely demolished in the XVI century, on an order by Grand Duke Cosimo I. It features a tower and some sections of the ancient walls. Its gardens overlook the central group of the towers of San Giminiano.

CHURCH OF SANT'AGOSTINO This Romanesque-gothic building (1280-98) features a very simple structure and a single nave. The choir features frescoes by Benozzo Gozzoli, such as the *Life of St Augustine* (1464-65), while the *Coronation of Mary* by Piero del Pollaiolo (1483) stands out on the main altar. Last but not least, the Chapel of San Bartolo houses a unique marble altar by Benedetto di Maiano (1494).

San Gimignano, Towers

OTHER INTERESTING PLACES

The surroundings of Siena are rich in towns and centres that are worth a visit. Due to space constraints, only some of them will be listed in what follows.

Abbadia San Salvatore,
Abbey

ABBADIA SAN SALVATORE This is an important summer and winter tourist resort. Erected on the south-east face of Mount Amiata, it was named after the important Benedictine Abbey, founded in 743 and only featuring the church and the crypt today. A must- see is the ABBEY OF SAN SALVATORE, also known as the abbey of Mount Amiata, founded in 743, under the reign of Rachis the Lombard. It soon grew so powerful that it became the richest Tuscan Abbey owned by the Benedictine Order, then by the Camaldolesian Order and finally, from 1228, by the Cistercian Order.

In 1782, Leopold I of Lorraine suppressed the abbey that, however, in 1939, was once again the seat of the Cistercians. The church, rebuilt in 1036 and enlarged at the end of the XIII century, was reworked in 1590 and entirely restored in 1968-71. Its one-nave interior features a rectory mounted at an elevation and a wonderful crypt with 36 column, probably dated VIII century. Next to the church is the monastery with its beautiful arcade, dating back to the first half of the XVII century. The town also includes a Medieval Borgo, artistically interesting, with gothic and renaissance buildings.

Buonconvento,
Town Hall

BUONCONVENTO This small agricultural town still preserves its medieval walls intact. The town was erected in the XIII century, near the ruins of the Percenna Castle, featuring a rectangular plan all surrounded by walls, that were, however, dismantled during the battle against Perugia. The new walls were erected in 1300 by the Sienese, who turned Buonconvento into an important defensive bastion. Here, Arrigo VII died on August 24, 1313. Worth visiting is the PARISH CHURCH OF SANTI PIETRO AND PAOLO, founded in the XIV century and entirely rebuilt in 1705. It houses interesting works of art. Also worth visiting is the PRAETORIAN PALACE, with its beautiful facade decorated with coat of arms and featuring a crenellated tower.

Castelnuovo Berardenga,
Charterhouse of Pontignano,
cloister

CASTELNUOVO BERARDENGA The town is famous for its wine. Here stand the ruins of a castle, built by the Sienese in 1366. Spending some time enjoying the landscape of this corner of the Sienese territory is a must.

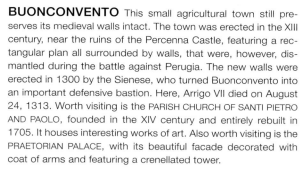

Close to Castelnuovo Berardenga rises this Charterhouse, today accommodating student housing facilities that date back to the XIV century. Through the first Renaissance cloister, featuring a well in the middle, and a XV-century portal, you can access a small XV-century cloister, surmounted by a loggia.

A third cloister, the largest, houses frescoes by Bernardino Poccetti under its vaults. This is the same artist that painted the frescoes of the church the first cloister opens onto. This church also features frescoes by other minor artists and is embellished by a wooden choir, carved by Domenico Atticciati, at the end of the XVI century.

SINALUNGA Situated on a hill, in the heart of the Valdichiana, it was originally known as Asinalunga, a name it has borne till 1864. During several centuries it remained under the rule of Siena, that, in 1399, relinquished it to Gian Galeazzo Visconti. From 1533, it passed into the hands of the Medici family and from then on its history and political events unfolded hand in hand with those of the rest of Tuscany, till the Unification of Italy.

COLLEGIATE CHURCH OF SAN MARTINO (Piazza Garibaldi) Its construction started in 1589. Its one-nave interior houses some beautiful painted panels, among which, on the altar in the left transept, a *Madonna with Child and Saints* by Sodoma.

PRAETORIAN PALACE (Piazza IV Novembre) This is a XIV-century building that was reworked several times. However, it still preserves a facade in Cotto tiles, decorated with stone coat of arms and surmounted by a beautiful Ghibelline tower.

Collegiate Church of San Martino, side chapels

Collegiate Church of San Martino

Sinalunga

itinerary

PRATO AND ITS SURROUNDINGS

del
one

na

a
oppi

Passo
dei Mandrioli

M. Fumaiolo
1407

Bibbiena

NO

larno

San Sepolcro

AREZZO

Castiglion
Fiorentino

Cortona

Lago
ontepulciano

ulciano

M. Cetona
1148

dia S. Salvatore

dente

PRATO
- DUOMO
- PIAZZA DEL COMUNE
- PALAZZO DATINI
- CHURCH OF SAN FRANCESCO
- CHURCH OF SANTA MARIA DELLE CARCERI
- CASTELLO DELL'IMPERATORE
- TEXTILE MUSEUM
- CENTRE FOR CONTEMPORARY ART L. PECCI

ITS SURROUNDINGS:
- FIGLINE
- VAIANO

PRATO

First evidence on the origins of the town dates back to the XI century, when a community settled around the parish church of Santo Stefano (today's Duomo). Already in the XII century, Prato was a free commune and a thriving town, prospering in mercantile trades and arts. From the first half of the XIII century, it became the seat of imperial vicars and entered the Ghibelline sphere of action of the Dagomari family. In 1267, the Guelphs went to power and, in order to suppress internal conflicts, the town placed itself under the protectorate of the Angioini Family of Naples. In 1351, Florence bought all rights over Prato from Queen Giovanna, at the price of 17,500

florins; therefore, though partially an autonomous town, Prato's history followed that of Florence from then onwards. The town is renowned for its textile and wool industry, first developed in the VIII century. Already in the XIII century its fine fabrics were sold all over Europe, thanks to its industrious artisans and to its skilled merchants; among these, worth remembering is Francesco di Marco Datini (approximately 1335-1410), who bequeathed his immense fortune to the poor. The so-called "regenerated wool", made from waste of knits and recycled textiles is also produced in Prato and it has been since 1880.

Prato, Duomo, facade,
Donatello and Michelozzo,
Pulpit of the Sacred Belt

DUOMO This is one of the most ancient churches in Prato: mention of it was found already in X-century documents, where it was referred to as Pieve di Santo Stefano. In the first half of the XIV century the church was enlarged, probably by Giovanni Pisano. The right angle of its facade features the superb *Pulpit of the Sacred Belt* by Donatello and Michelozzo (1428-38). The bell tower was erected at the beginning of the XIII century and equipped with a bell chamber between 1340 and 1356. The cathedral features a triple-nave interior, accommodating the pulpit by Mino da Fiesole and Bernardo Rossellino (1473). The Chapel of the Sacred Belt (first chapel on the left as you enter the cathedral), built between 1385 and 1395, houses the magnificent frescoes by Agnolo Gaddi (1392-95), depicting *Scenes from the legend of the Sacred Belt*. Legend has it that the Virgin Mary gave her belt to St Thomas on her ascending into Heaven and that St Thomas gave it to a priest, a descendent of whom married Michele Dagomari from Prato and brought the precious relic as her dowry. The MUSEUM OF THE OPERA DEL DUOMO houses the original panels by Donatello, made for the pulpit of the Sacred Belt, besides other valuable works of art, dated XIII-XVII centuries.

PIAZZA DEL COMUNE This square contains the *Fountain of Bacchino* by Ferdinando Tacca (1659), a symbol of the town, and is also overlooked by the PRAETORIAN PALACE. Built between the XIII and the XIV century, the palace features battlements and a bell tower dating back to the XVI century and also accommodates the GALLERIA COMUNALE, housing paintings that are mainly from the XIV- and XV-century Florentine school. The original XIV-century appearance of the Town Hall has been altered by the current classical facade, erected by Giuseppe Valentini and dating back to the end of the XVIII century.

PALAZZO DATINI (Via Ser Lapo Mazzei) This was the house where Francesco di Marco Datini lived (1335-1410); he was one

Prato, Duomo

of the most important bankers and merchants of his time. The house, still retaining its original architectural and decorative elements, is the seat of an historical archive, housing 140,000 account books and business letters by the house master.

CHURCH OF SAN FRANCESCO (Piazza San Francesco) Built at the end of the XIII century, this Church was later embellished with Renaissance elements. It features a single-nave interior. On the floor across the presbytery lies the *tomb slab of Francesco Datini*, carved by Niccolò Lamberti in 1411.

Church of San Francesco

CHURCH OF SANTA MARIA DELLE CARCERI (Piazza delle Carceri) It was built to house a miraculous image of the Virgin Mary, previously placed outside the jail, hence its name. Lorenzo de Medici charged Giuliano da Sangallo (1484-95) with carrying out the works, and the latter erected a church featuring a Greek-cross plan, inspired to the Cappella dei Pazzi by Filippo Brunelleschi. Its interior houses the *Medallions with the Evangelists*, in enamelled terracotta, by Andrea della Robbia (circa1490).

Church of Santa Maria
delle Carceri

CASTELLO DELL'IMPERATORE also known as the FORTRESS OF SANTA BARBARA (Piazza delle Carceri) It was built for Frederick II and erected between 1237 and 1248. It is a unique monument in both central and northern Italy and is very similar to Swabian castles, as well as to the castles of Sicily and Apulia.

TEXTILE MUSEUM (Viale della Repubblica) This is a very peculiar museum, displaying old machineries and valuable fabrics of all ages, proving evidence of the long tradition of Prato textile industry, that made the town famous worldwide.

CENTRE FOR CONTEMPORARY ART LUIGI PEC-CI (Viale della Repubblica) The building, erected in 1988, accommodates the Museum of Contemporary Art. It is also used for concerts, motion pictures and exhibitions.

Castello dell'Imperatore

THE SURROUNDINGS OF PRATO

Near Prato, whether travelling North (Bologna), North-East, or West (Pistoia and the coastline), you will find noteworthy natural spots, along with small towns that retain relevant artistic evidence. Among these are:

FIGLINE This small town has been renowned since antiquity for its terracotta production (referred to as *figulinae* in Latin, hence the name of the town).
The Parish church of Santo Stefano stands out for its elegant bell tower, featuring single- and double-lancet windows. Its interior houses XIV-century frescoes.

Museum Luigi Pecci

VAIANO This small town holds important evidence of its past history. The most relevant monument is the CHURCH OF SAN SALVATORE, with a bell tower built in 1258, featuring two levels of double-lancet windows, a sacristy with remarkable woodcarving works dating back to the XVIII century, besides a large XV-century cloister: this is what remains of the Abbey of San Salvatore, founded by the Benedictine monks in 1073.

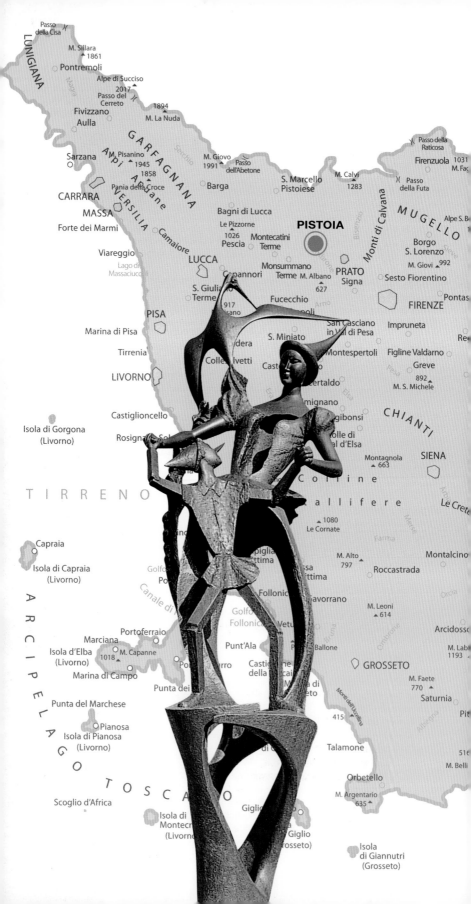

itinerary

7

PISTOIA AND ITS SURROUNDINGS

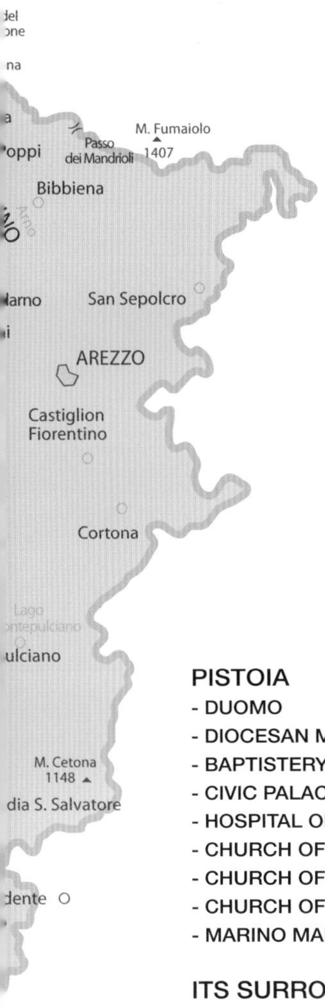

M. Fumaiolo
1407
Passo dei Mandrioli
Bibbiena
San Sepolcro
AREZZO
Castiglion Fiorentino
Cortona
M. Cetona
1148

PISTOIA

- DUOMO
- DIOCESAN MUSEUM
- BAPTISTERY
- CIVIC PALACES
- HOSPITAL OF CEPPO
- CHURCH OF SAN BARTOLOMEO IN PANTANO
- CHURCH OF SAN GIOVANNI FUORICIVITAS
- CHURCH OF SAN ANDREA
- MARINO MARINI CENTRE

ITS SURROUNDINGS:

- ABETONE
- BUGGIANO
- MONTECATINI TERME
- MONSUMMANO TERME
- PESCIA
- COLLODI
- CUTIGLIANO
- DOGANACCIA
- MASSA AND COZZILE
- RIVORETA

PISTOIA

The origins of Pistoia probably date back to the II century B.C. During the Middle Ages it was a military stronghold and, when Countess Matilda died (1115), Pistoia proclaimed itself a free, Ghibelline Commune, hence it had to face vicious wars against Florence, Lucca and Prato, which, however, did not prevent it from developing into an important commercial, industrial and agricultural town. In the XIII century, Pistoia experienced its most splendid age; it was provided with fortified walls and 60 towers, which, however, could not prevent it from being caught between the opposing powers of Florence and Lucca. Despite an enlargement of the city walls in 1314, the town was forced to sign a peace treaty with Florence in 1329, so as to restore its activities.

In 1530 Pistoia permanently entered the Florentine sphere of influence, for it had been included in the new Duchy, that Pope Clement VII had founded to install his nephew Alessandro de' Medici. From then on Pistoia shared the same fate as Tuscany: in 1737, the city was taken over by the Grand Dukes of Lorraine; then it was under the French domination, after which, in 1859, it became part of the Kingdom of Italy together with Tuscany. Unfortunately, during World War II, Pistoia's artistic heritage was largely damaged. Where possible, buildings have been restored; however, this was not always feasible, as in the case of the demolished Church of San Giovanni Battista.

Duomo

DUOMO The original nucleus of this cathedral was erected in the V century, to be later entirely rebuilt in a XII- and XIII-century Pisan Romanesque style. Its facade features a barrel vault in the centre, with enamelled-terracotta coffers by Andrea della Robbia, and a lunette with a bas-relief, depicting the *Madonna with*

Duomo, interior

Child between two Angels, situated over the central portal (1505). Resting on its left flank is the bell tower (67 m.), erected as a Lombard watchtower and added with three storeys at the end of the XIII century. The church interior, with its three naves, houses many works of art, among which is the *Tomb of Cino da Pistoia*, a friend of Dante's, depicted while teaching to his pupils. Cellino di Nese was commissioned the tomb, but he had a Sienese master build it in 1337. Worth mentioning is the *Chapel of San Jacopo*, housing the Altar or altar frontal of San Jacopo (a panel, made of stone or other material, erected behind the altar and dominating it), one of the most relevant works by Italian goldsmiths, composed of 628 figures; started in 1287, it was finished in 1456. Almost all Italian goldsmiths worked at it, including Filippo Brunelleschi, before he decided to dedicate himself to architecture alone.

DIOCESAN MUSEUM Accommodated in the Palazzo Vescovile, near the Duomo, it houses crucifixes, reliquaries and chalices, made between the XIII and the XV centuries by local artists.

BAPTISTERY Construction of the Baptistery started in 1337 and was completed in 1361, carried out by Cellino di Nese, to the design, according to Vasari, of Andrea Pisano.
It is entirely covered with white and green marble. The baptistery has lost its liturgical function today and occasionally houses cultural events.

CIVIC PALACES To the right of the Baptistery is the PALAZZO DEL PODESTÀ, also referred to as the PRAETORIAN PALACE. It was erected as an austere building in 1367 and enlarged in 1844-46. Today it accommodates the Court. Opposite the Praetorian Palace stands the TOWN HALL, built by the Guelphs in 1294 and enlarged over the centuries that followed. It accommodates the CIVIC MUSEUM, housing works of art ranging from the Middle Ages to the XX century.

HOSPITAL OF CEPPO (Piazza Giovanni XXIII) Named after the dry trunk ("ceppo") where all alms were collected, the hospital was probably erected in 1277 and later brought under the control of the Hospital of Santa Maria Nova in Florence, therefore, a Florentine was appointed as its "spedalingo" (hospital rector). Its facade is embellished by the presence of an arcade in a Florentine style and by an enamelled-terracotta decoration, made in the Della Robbia's workshop (1514-25).

Town Hall, courtyard

CHURCH OF SAN BARTOLOMEO IN PANTANO (Piazza San Bartolomeo) Built in 1159, the Church was named such for it had been erected on a swamp. It houses the superb *pulpit* by Guido da Como (1250), shaped as a rectangular structure resting on three columns and decorated with bas-reliefs: it characterised the passage from the Romanesque art of Pistoia into the great art of Giovanni Pisano.

CHURCH OF SAN GIOVANNI FUORICIVITAS (Via Cavour) The church was named such for it was erected outside the city walls. Its first nucleus dates back to the VIII century, whereas the actual building was started in the mid XII century and completed in the XIV century. Its one-nave interior houses the beautiful *font* by the young Giovanni Pisano and the *pulpit* by Guglielmo da Pisa, disciple of Nicola Pisano, completed in 1270 and depicting scenes from the Old Testament.

Church of S. Andrea, Giovanni Pisano, pulpit

CHURCH OF SAN ANDREA (Via San Andrea) The Church features a beautiful facade in a Pisan style, built in the XII century. Its interior, divided into three narrow naves, houses a *Baptismal Font*, probably by Giovanni Pisano, and, most importantly, the *pulpit* by Giovanni Pisano (1298-1301), considered to be one of the masterpieces of Italian sculptural tradition. It features an hexagonal structure, resting on seven columns and decorated with *scenes from the life of Jesus Christ*, along with statues depicting sibyls and prophets.

MARINO MARINI CENTRE (Corso Silvano Fedi) This museum is dedicated to the sculptor Marino Marini (1901-80), the most famous modern artist from Pistoia. It houses the drawings and sculptures that dotted the journey through which the master developed his style: an artistic evolution that started with a naturalist style to culminate in the revival of the ancient style and beyond, to access the universe of abstract art.

THE SURROUNDINGS OF PISTOIA

Abetone

ABETONE A summer and winter resort, the town is situated at an height of 1388 metres, amidst the fir-woods, on the Apennines at the border between Tuscany and Emilia Romagna. The town took its name from a huge fir-tree that was cut down in the XIX century to build the road connecting Tuscany with Romagna. Two stone pyramids were erected here to celebrate this ingenious work, built for the kings of Modena and Tuscany, Francesco II of Este and Leopold II of Lorraine. Abetone, renowned ski-resort, is equipped with several cableways to reach the well-organised cabins, from where you can reach the sky trails or simply enjoy the wonderful landscape, such as L'Alpe delle Tre Potenze (1940 m.), named such because the place once signed the border between the Grand Duchy of Tuscany and the Duchy of Modena and Lucca, or Mount Cimone (2165 m.), offering, during clear days, panoramic views of the Tyrrhenian and the Adriatic coasts.

Buggiano, Praetorian Palace

BUGGIANO The town is divided into Buggiano Castello on top of the hill and Borgo a Buggiano down in the valley. The hilly area still maintains a medieval aspect, especially in the Piazzetta della Pieve, dominated by the PRAETORIAN PALACE, also known as Palazzo del Podestà, dating back to the XII century and featuring a beautiful facade. It was restored a few decades ago, thus saving its remarkable Renaissance coat of arms from further deterioration. Still in this square, the visitor will find the PIEVE ROMANICA, a Romanesque Parish Church built in 1308 as a Benedictine Abbey and reworked during the Renaissance period. Its triple-nave interior contains several XII- to XVII-century artworks.

Montecatini Terme

MONTECATINI TERME The town was already renowned as a spa resort at the time of the Romans, who appreciated the therapeutic properties of its salt-sulphated waters. It enjoyed great prosperity under Grand Duke Pietro Leopoldo (1780), who

Montecatini,
Tettuccio Thermal Resort

built the first thermal facilities, each one erected on a water spring, with water being channelled into fountains and pools. Montecatini is still today one of the most famous spa resort in Europe, where, besides drinking water, tourists are offered a full range of beauty treatments. Among the most renowned spa resorts are the Terme Leopoldine, built in 1775 and rebuilt in 1925, reproducing a Classical-Temple architecture; the Terme Tettuccio, built between 1925 and 1928, featuring fountains, pools, music halls in an Art Nouveau style; the Terme Torretta, also famous for housing concerts at tea time, and the Terme Tamerici, featuring awesome gardens. Also in Montecatini are the Terme Regina, Terme Rinfresco, Terme Giulia, each specialised in the treatment of different diseases.

Montecatini,
Torretta Thermal Resort

Montecatini, Tamerici Thermal Resort

MONSUMMANO TERME
The town, not too far from Montecatini, is famous for its natural thermal grottoes, the most renowned of which is the Grotta Giusti with its thermal steam-baths.

Pescia, Duomo

Pescia, Church of San Francesco,
Bonaventura Berlinghieri,
St Francis and scenes
from his life

PESCIA This is an important town in the Valdinievole, surrounded by greenhouses producing flowers that are sold in the biggest wholesale mart of Italy; besides floriculture, Pescia is also developing a nursery industry.

The town underwent a peculiar urban subdivision, divided as it is in five districts, known as "quinti", which led to developing its religious centre all around Piazza del Duomo, on the left bank of river Pescia, and its administrative centre all around the actual Piazza Mazzini. Originally under the rule of Lucca, the town passed under the Florentine domination in 1329, thus intertwining its history to that of Florence, till the Unification of Italy.

DUOMO Dedicated to Santa Maria Assunta, it is a Baroque remake of the ancient parish church of Santa Maria. It was rebuilt several times and given its actual structure in 1684, when the original Latin Cross structure was substituted with a single nave. Its facade, added at the end of 1800, is by Giuseppe Castellucci. This was only completed in 1933, with the addition of a marble portal. The Cathedral interior features the outstanding Turini Chapel and the Bishops' Chapel.

CHURCH OF SAN FRANCESCO Built in 1298 on an ancient oratory dating back to 1211, probably donated by Venanzio Orlandi to St Francis, the Church was enlarged in the XVI and in the XVII centuries. Its interior, restored some decades ago, houses several works of art, among which stands out the beautiful table on the third altar on the right, depicting *St Francis and scenes from his life*, painted by Bonaventura Berlinghieri in 1235.

Apparently, the artist knew the Saint from Assisi and, therefore, the portrait is believed to be adherent to reality. Besides this, the church also houses other valuable Renaissance works of art.

PALAZZO DEI VICARI (Piazza Mazzini) This magnificent building, dating back to the XIII-XIV century, features a facade decorated with several coat of arms. Today it accommodates the local government.

PALAZZO GALEOTTI (Piazza Mazzini) Built at the beginning of 1700 in a late Baroque style, it accommodates the Civic Museum, displaying a collection of works from the local churches and from private collections. Among these is a *Virgin and Child between Saints Peter and Stephen* by Lorenzo Monaco, and an *Annunciation and Coronation of the Virgin Mary* by Neri di Bicci.

VALDINIEVOLE ARCHAEOLOGICAL MUSEUM (Piazza Leonardo da Vinci) The Museum houses artefacts from prehistory to 1800, found in the archaeological sites of the Valdinievole.

COLLODI The Florentine author of Pinocchio, Carlo Lorenzini (1826-90), adopted the name of his mother's hometown as his pseudonym, thus making this small town famous worldwide. In 1956, the town of Collodi dedicated a park to the wooden puppet, that has welcomed plenty of curious visitors over the years. Here you can find reproductions of the *Monument of Pinocchio* by Emilio Greco, along with all the characters in the fairy tale written in 1881, all by great artists. The beautiful Villa Garzoni is situated in Collodi. Built between 1633 and 1662, it is surrounded by a garden decorated with statues and fountains with water jets, where the geometry of a Renaissance taste melts with the beauty of Baroque creations.

Collodi, Emilio Greco, Monument to Pinocchio

CUTIGLIANO This is a nice summer and winter resort, immersed in the woods of Pistoia mountains. The town centre hosts the XIV-century PRAETORIAN PALACE, erected by the seven biggest mountain towns (Lizzano, San Marcello, Cutigliano, Popiglio, Piteglio, Gavinana and Mammiano), featuring a facade decorated with some glazed-terracotta coat of arms by Della Robbia (beginning of the XVI century).

DOGANACCIA (m. 1540) From Cutigliano, by both cableway or by road, you will reach this charming place, with its many ski trails, equipped cabins and its renowned skiing school.

Cozzile, medieval-style building designed by G. Paciarelli

MASSA AND COZZILE A few kilometres away from Buggiano Castello is the town of Massa, seat of Massa and Cozzile's local government. Massa still hosts the PALAZZO DEL PODESTA', a palace that has repeatedly undergone modifications and finally became a private house. Seven Km away from Massa is the town of Cozzile, situated on the highest spot of an area surrounded by shady woods. Worth visiting here is the villa that is actually a medieval-like castle, built in the XIX century.

RIVORETA At an altitude of 900 m. lies the pleasant holiday resort known as Rivoreta, hosting a peculiar ethnological museum, displaying objects and tools that illustrate rural culture. It was built on the ancient road connecting Cutigliano and Fiumalbo. Its main square is dominated by the XIX-century, neo-gothic church, with a facade featuring four pilasters.

itinerary

8

AREZZO AND ITS SURROUNDINGS

del
one

na

a

'oppi
Passo
dei Mandrioli

M. Fumaiolo
▲ 1407

Bibbiena

Iarno

San Sepolcro

AREZZO

Castiglion
Fiorentino

Cortona

Lago
antepulciano

ulciano

M. Cetona
1148 ▲

dia S. Salvatore

dente

AREZZO
- BASILICA OF SAN FRANCESCO
- PARISH CHURCH OF SANTA MARIA
- PIAZZA GRANDE
- PRAETORIAN PALACE
- THE TOWN HALL
- CHURCH OF SAN DOMENICO
- VASARI'S HOUSE
- MEDICEAN FORTRESS
- STATE ART MUSEUM
- ROMAN AMPHITHEATRE
- ARCHAEOLOGICAL MUSEUM
- CHURCH OF SANTA MARIA DELLE GRAZIE

ITS SURROUNDINGS:
- ANGHIARI
- CASTIGLION FIORENTINO
- CORTONA
- LUCIGNANO
- MONTE SAN SAVINO
- SANSEPOLCRO
- LA VERNA SANCTUARY
- MONASTERY OF THE CARTHUSIAN MONKS
- CAPRESE MICHELANGELO
- CASENTINO FOREST
- POPPI
- STIA
- PIAN DI SCO'
- PIEVE DI SANTO STEFANO

AREZZO

The Etruscan *Arretimu* was an important boomtown,
deemed to have been surrounded by walls already in the IV
century B.C. It expanded considerably under Roman rule,
in the I century B.C., to the point that its walls had to be
enlarged to contain all the newly erected buildings.
In the XII century, under the rule of the count-bishops, the
city walls were further enlarged and Arezzo enjoyed a period
of remarkable economic and demographic development.
Around 1200, the city became a commune and new
encompassing walls were erected, which connected to the
Etruscan-Roman walls to the North-East. It was by then
that conflicts between Siena and Florence embittered,
which caused a surge of death and destruction that lasted
over several years. On June 11, 1289, Arezzo was finally
defeated by Florence at Campaldino. In 1312, Bishop Guido
Tarlati was appointed lifelong lord of the city. Under his rule,
the city was temporarily restored to its prestige, which led
to further enlarging the city walls in 1317.

When Bishop Tarlati died, however, the fortunes of Arezzo rapidly ebbed and the city was sold twice, in 1337 and in 1384, and eventually succumbed to Florentine domination. From then on its history was subsumed by that of the more powerful Florence: Cosimo I de' Medici asked Antonio da Sangallo to supply Arezzo with a new defence system, envisaging new bastioned city-walls, erected between 1538 and 1560 (unfortunately demolished around 1870s), mainly consisting on restoring the ancient Fortress, and only slightly rearranging the perspective of the XIV-century structure. After a period of decay under the rule of the Grand Duchy, Arezzo permanently re-established its status with the Unification of Italy, especially due to the construction of the Florence-Rome railway (1862-66), dramatically boosting the city expansion.

Basilica of San Francesco
Main Altar, Master Painter of
St Francis (a contemporary
of Cimabue's), crucifix
in the background:
Piero della Francesca,
Scenes from the Legend of
the True Cross

BASILICA OF SAN FRANCESCO (Piazza San Francesco) First built in the mid XIII century, it eventually underwent massive renovation and evolved into an Umbrian-Tuscan Gothic church in the years 1318-1377. The bell tower was added in the XVI century. Its interior is made of a single nave, flanked by niches on the right and by chapels on the left. The choir (used by choristers and arranged beneath the main altar) houses a fresco cycle among the most beautiful of all Renaissance frescoes, probably the highest expression of all artistic production. It features the *Legends of the True Cross*, painted by Piero della Francesca between 1453 and 1464. Piero illustrated the story of Jesus' Cross, cut in the wood from the tree which grew the forbidden fruit Eve picked to tempt Adam. Legend has it that Empress Elena found the wood near Jerusalem, and that her son Constantine transformed it into a war emblem (in 313, he issued the Edict of Milan, legalising Christian worship). Narration starts on the upper right part of the wall, according to the following sequence: 1) *Death and burial of Adam;* 2) *The Queen of Sheba in adoration of the bridge and the meeting of the Queen of Sheba with Solomon;* 3) *Removal of the bridge;* 4) *Constantine's dream;* 5) *Victory of Constantine in the battle against Maxentius;* 6) *Torture and confession of Jude the Jew;* 7) *Discovery and proof of the true Cross;* 8) *Victory of Heraclius in the battle against the Persian king Chosroes;* 9) *Heraclius returning the Cross to Jerusalem;* 10-11) *Two Prophets;* 12) *Annunciation.*

PARISH CHURCH OF SANTA MARIA (Corso Italia) This is one of the most beautiful Romanesque churches in Tuscany. Built after 1140, maybe over a pre-existing church, it was renovated in the XVI century by Vasari. Its facade dates back to the XIII century and features a complex tangle of arches and sculptures. Its bell tower, built in 1330, is known as "the hundred-hole bell tower", due to its 40 double-lancet windows (such are called those windows divided in two section by the presence of a mullion). Its interior, altered by XIX-century restoration works, features three naves and houses the *Polittico* by Pietro Lorenzetti (1320) along with the *Madonna with Child and four Saints*, the *Annunciation* and *Our Lady of Assumption and twelve Saints* just above the main altar.

Pieve di Santa Maria,
Middle nave

Piazza Grande

PIAZZA GRANDE Erected in the XIII century, it underwent modifications during the XVI century. It is overlooked by the PALACE OF THE LAY FRATERNITY raised on a flight of steps dating back to 1780. It was built between 1375 and 1377, though its facade was completed in 1434 by Bernardo Rossellino, who also authored the beautiful bas-relief in a lunette, on the facade. In 1552, the bell tower known as CAMPANILETTO was added, featuring a clock showing days along with the phases of the moon and the motion of the sun. On this same square stands the PALAZZO DELLE LOGGE, designed by Vasari in 1573, with its porch still hosting ancient-style workshops.

PRAETORIAN PALACE (Via Pilcati) Its original structure dates back to the late XIV century; it underwent modifications during the XVI century, was restored in 1933-34 and nowadays accommodates the town LIBRARY.

THE TOWN HALL (Piazza della Libertà) It was built in 1333 as the Priors' Palace. Unfortunately, its original structure has been altered, due to heavy restoration interventions. The top of its tower, dating back to 1337, was restored with the palace; it is decorated by a clock that dates back to1468.

CHURCH OF SAN DOMENICO (Piazza Fossombroni) Founded in 1275 by the Tarlati family of Pietramala, maybe to a design by Nicola Pisano, the Church underwent many reshapings throughout the centuries. It has a single-nave interior. The *Crucifix* on the main altar is a masterpiece by the young Cimabue (1260-65), along with being one of the first iconographic representations of Jesus Christ.

VASARI'S HOUSE (Via XX Settembre) Giorgio Vasari (1512-74), who was born in Arezzo, built this dwelling for himself between 1540 and 1548. He designed it, equipped it with furniture and frescoed it together with his painter friends, thus making it a perfect example of a Manneristic Tuscan residence. Besides being an architect, Vasari was also a painter.

His famous book *The lives of the most excellent Italian painters, sculptors and architects from Cimabue to our times* (1550), in which he describes the artistic productions of many great artists, has made him the first art historian.

Town Hall

Church of San Domenico, interior

MEDICEAN FORTRESS Built on pre-existing fortifications of the XIV century, the fortress was later reshaped by Giuliano and Antonio da Sangallo during the second half of the XVI century for Cosimo I. Partly dismantled by the French, it was first restored in 1868, while also successively reworked in more recent times. Its bastions offer a beautiful panorama.

STATE MEDIEVAL AND MODERN ART MUSEUM (Via di San Lorenzino) Accommodated in the beautiful Palazzo Bruni-Ciocchi, it was probably designed by Bernardo Rossellino in 1445. This museum was the result of the fusion between the Town Art Gallery and the Laymen's Brotherhood Museum and displays collections of majolicas, along with minor artworks and a wide range of paintings dating back to a time-span ranging from the XIII to the XIX century.

THE ROMAN AMPHITHEATRE AND THE ARCHAEOLOGICAL MUSEUM (Via Margaritone) The elliptic amphitheatre is comprised of two orders of tiers. It was built between the end of the I and the beginning of the II century A.D. Next to the Roman ruins there is the museum, housed in the former Monastery of San Bernardo, displaying a wide collection of Arezzo's prehistoric, Etruscan and Roman artefacts. Most interesting is the collection of *coral vases*, a type of coral-red pottery that was produced between the I century B.C. and the I century A.D. and exported throughout the Roman Empire.

Church of San Domenico, Cimabue, wooden Christ

Church of Santa Maria delle Grazie

CHURCH OF SANTA MARIA DELLE GRAZIE (Via di Santa Maria) The Church was built between 1435 and 1444. Around 1490, a porch was added to the project by Benedetto da Maiano. Its small interior has a single nave, with an almost unique main altar by Andrea della Robbia (1435-1528?), made of marble (a building material the artist only rarely resorted to) and enamelled terracotta, with a fresco by Parri di Spinello (1430) featuring *Our Lady of Mercy*.

THE SURROUNDINGS OF AREZZO

Anghiari, Church of Sant' Agostino

ANGHIARI It is an ancient hilltown still surrounded by its medieval walls. It is situated on a rocky spur in the Tiber Valley (close to Mount Fumaiolo, where the Tiber river rises). Its ancient quarter is made up of medieval small houses overlooking a maze of tiny squares and alleys. The small town was first known in the XI century for being the battlefield where the Florentine and the Papal armies fought their most important battle against Milan army on June 29, 1440; with Florence winning the battle, Anghiari yielded to the Florentine dominion. A must see is the CHURCH OF BADIA (San Bartolomeo Apostolo). Founded soon after the year 1000, it underwent quite a few transformations, but still houses works of art dating back to the XV and the XVI centuries. Also worth visiting is the TAGLIESCHI PALACE, a Renaissance building accommodating the State Museum of Arts and Popular Traditions of the upper Tiber Valley, with its display of utensils and agricultural implements, along with major artworks, followed by the CHURCH OF SANT' AGOSTINO, erected in the XII century and rebuilt in the XV century. Its single-nave interior houses XV- and XVI-century artworks.

Anghiari, an alley

CASTIGLION FIORENTINO This is a small town surrounded by XIII- and XIV-century walls, as well as by a number of towers dating back to the XIV and XV centuries, on which the ancient donjon was erected. In 1014, it was still known as *Castiglione Aretino*, though, due to the political events that followed, it came under the rule of Florence and was renamed Castiglion Fiorentino. In Piazza del Municipio, the XVI-century CANNALE PALACE, largely rebuilt in 1935, is partially dedicated to the Civic Art Gallery, housing XIII- to XVI-century artworks. Also in this square are the arcades known as LOGGE DEL VASARI. Built in 1560, the arcades feature nine arches supported by pillars of pietra serena, with a number of coats of arms decorating their walls. The Romanesque-Gothic CHURCH OF SAN FRANCESCO was built during the second half of the XIII century and houses, in its single-nave interior, a panel by Margaritone d'Arezzo, depicting *St Francis* and painted between 1280 and 1290; besides this, the church also displays a number of XIV-century frescoes. The ancient XV-century parish church leans against the collegiate CHURCH OF SAN GIULIANO, newly built between 1840 and 1853 and preserving a valuable terracotta from the workshops of Della Robbia.

Town Art Gallery, anonymous artist of the early XIII century, painted Cross

Cortona coat of arms, Florence, Cappella dei Principi

CORTONA It was renowned as an Etruscan town under the name of *Corita* (V century B.C.); still surrounded by what is left of its mighty walls, the city was conquered by Rome in 89 B.C. and was destroyed by the Goths in 450 A.D. After an absolute lack of documentation, the city is again cited in documents dating back to the XI century, when it finally restored its fortunes and achieved its maximum splendour, namely after 1411, when it came under the rule of Florence and its history was subsumed to that of Florence for the following centuries. Cortona was hometown to the painters Luca Signorelli (1441-1523) and Pietro Berrettini (1596-1669), known as Pietro from Cortona.

DUOMO (Piazza del Duomo) Built to the design of Giuliano da Sangallo in the XVI century, the Cathedral was built on a pre-existing, ancient Roman abbey, the remains of which are still visible in its facade. Its bell tower was designed by Francesco Laparelli in 1566.

A beautiful portal designed in 1550 by Cristofanello provides access to the cathedral three-nave interior, with its XVI- and XVIII-century paintings and sculptures.

DIOCESAN MUSEUM (Piazza del Duomo) Set up inside the Chiesa del Gesù (1498-1505), the Diocesan Museum is certainly a must-see; among the works on display here are the *Annunciation* by Beato Angelico (1428-30), a *Deposition* by Luca Signorelli and a *Crucifixion* by Pietro Lorenzetti (1280-1348).

Cortona, Diocesan Museum, Beato Angelico, Annunciation

ETRUSCAN ACADEMY MUSEUM (Piazza Signorelli) This is an interesting museum housing ancient Egyptian, Etruscan and Roman finds, besides displaying paintings and objects for a time span ranging from the XIII to the XIX century. The most famous object on display here is the *Etruscan bronze Chandelier* dating back to the V century B.C.; found in a field in 1840, it is unique in its kind (with a diameter of 60 cm, it weighs 57.72 kg). Also on display here is the peculiar *Egyptian funerary boat* dated to the II millennium B.C. The museum has its seat in the Praetorian Palace, built in the XIII century for the Casali family and restored in 1613 by Filippo Berrettini.

Cortona, Etruscan Academy Museum, Bronze Candelabrum

CHURCH OF SAN FRANCESCO (Via Maffei) Built in 1245 by Friar Elia Cappi, successor of St Francis in leading the Order, this Church features a simple structure that stands on a majestic flight of steps. It was partially remodelled both internally and externally in the XVII century and houses the *Annunciation*, the last and unfinished work by Pietro da Cortona, a *Byzantine Reliquary of the Holy Cross*, dated to the X century, which Friar Elia brought from Constantinople, where Fredrick II had sent him as his ambassador. Both Friar Elia and Luca Signorelli are buried in this church.

SANCTUARY OF SANTA MARGHERITA An uphill road with gardens on both sides leads to the Church. Designed by the Futurist Artist Gino Severini (1883-1966) and meant to be a war memorial, the road is decorated with mosaics featuring the Stations of the Cross (the *Passion*) to indicate the way to the Sanctuary. Built on a medieval Church, this sanctuary was reconstructed between 1856 and 1897 and underwent considerable Roman-Gothic transformations. Its modern three-nave interior houses ancient artworks, such as the marble *tomb of St Margaret*, sculptured in 1362 by Angelo and Francesco di Pietro.

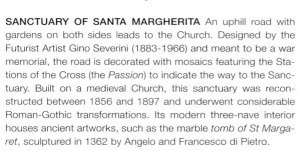

Cortona, Church of San Francesco, interior

Must-see are also: SAN NICCOLÒ (Via San Niccolò), a small XV-century church; SAN DOMENICO (Largo Beato Angelico), a late-Gothic-style Church; the MEDICEAN FORTRESS, built for the Medici family in the XVI century; the MANCINI-SERNINI PALACE, built in 1533 by Cristofanello, and Via Janelli, with its medieval houses, among the best preserved on the whole Italian territory, featuring jetties supported by cantilevered timber beams.

Cortona, Church of Santa
Maria delle Grazie

Cortona, Church of Santa
Maria delle Grazie, interior

Lucignano
Church of San Francesco

Monte San Savino, Porta
Fiorentina

Monte San Savino, Museum
of Folk Ceramics

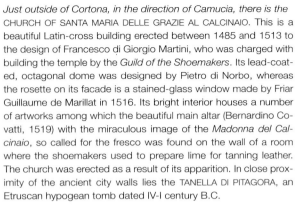

Just outside of Cortona, in the direction of Camucia, there is the CHURCH OF SANTA MARIA DELLE GRAZIE AL CALCINAIO. This is a beautiful Latin-cross building erected between 1485 and 1513 to the design of Francesco di Giorgio Martini, who was charged with building the temple by the *Guild of the Shoemakers*. Its lead-coated, octagonal dome was designed by Pietro di Norbo, whereas the rosette on its facade is a stained-glass window made by Friar Guillaume de Marillat in 1516. Its bright interior houses a number of artworks among which the beautiful main altar (Bernardino Covatti, 1519) with the miraculous image of the *Madonna del Calcinaio*, so called for the fresco was found on the wall of a room where the shoemakers used to prepare lime for tanning leather. The church was erected as a result of its apparition. In close proximity of the ancient city walls lies the TANELLA DI PITAGORA, an Etruscan hypogean tomb dated IV-I century B.C.

LUCIGNANO It is a small town overlooking the Valdichiana; elliptical in shape, it is a unique example of medieval town planning strategies.

COLLEGIATE CHURCH OF SAN MICHELE Raised on a flight of circular steps, the church was built in 1594 by Orazio Porta. Its single-nave interior houses some remarkable XVIII-century wood-sculptures.

THE TOWN HALL A section of the XIV-century Town Hall accommodates the City Museum, displaying an interesting collection of paintings, among which the *Madonna with Child and Saints* by Luca Signorelli. Also displayed here is the so-called *St Francis' Tree*, also known as *Lucignano's Tree*, a gold reliquary that stands out as a masterpiece of Siena Goldsmiths. Started by Ugolino di Vieri (1350), it was completed by Gabriello d'Antonio in 1471.

CHURCH OF SAN FRANCESCO Built in the XIII century, this church features a Romanic facade with a Gothic portal in the middle. Its single-nave interior houses remarkable remains of frescoes by XIV-century Sienese artists.

MONTE SAN SAVINO Situated in the West Val di Chiana, the town was long disputed by Arezzo and Florence, with the latter permanently extending its dominion on it. It was hometown to Andrea Contucci, known as Sansovino (1460/67-1529), famous architect and sculptor, whose works are still visible testimonies of his artistic activity in town. Must-see are: PORTA FIORENTINA, a XVI-century remake, to a design by Vasari, of an ancient gate of the town walls, portions of which are still standing; the CERAMIC MUSEUM (Piazza Ganurrini), displaying the local ceramic production also at the centre of a town festival to be held at Spring; the LOGGIA DEI MERCANTI (Corso Sangallo), an example of Renaissance architecture either by Antonio da Sangallo the Old or by Andrea Sansovino (1518-20), made up of five arcades supported by elegant fluted columns, surmounted by Corinthian capitals; THE TOWN HALL (Corso Sangallo), in a Florentine Renaissance style, built to the design of Sangallo the Old in 1515 for Cardinal Del Monte. Piazza di Monte is also overlooked by the house that was the birthplace of Sansovino, who designed both the square and the beautiful arcade opposite the CHURCH OF SANT'AGOSTINO. Built in the XIV century, it was eventually reworked and enlarged in the XVI and in the XVIII centuries. Its single-nave interior houses XIV- and XV-century frescoes, along with the altarpiece painted by Vasari, signed and dated 1539. Sansovino was buried here, behind the pulpit, his tomb slab showing signs of the passing of time.

SANSEPOLCRO

SANSEPOLCRO The town is probably named after the Oratory built in 934 to house the relics from the Holy Sepulcre, which two pilgrims brought on their way back from the Holy Land. Around it mushroomed the village that, after several political events, was eventually sold to Florence in 1441. It was hometown to the famous painter Piero della Francesca (circa 1420-92), whose production is partially housed in the CIVIC MUSEUM, inside the XIV-century TOWN HALL. The most famous artwork displayed here is the *Resurrection*, a fresco painted in 1463, dominated by the mighty presence of Jesus Christ; besides this, the place also displays *Our Lady of Mercy and Saints*, a panel of a dismembered polyptych, painted after 1445.

Sansepolcro, Piazza di Berta

DUOMO This Roman-Gothic Cathedral is dedicated to San Giovanni Evangelista. Started during the first half of the year 1000, the building underwent many transformations over the centuries and up to 1859, to be partially reverted to the original structure and style in the XX century.

PALAZZO DELLE LAUDI Seat of the Town Hall, this palace is a Manneristic building by Alberto Alberti, built in 1595.

MEDICEAN FORTRESS Probably planned by Alberto Alberti in the XVI century, to the design by Giuliano da Sangallo, it is considered a remarkable example of military architecture.

SANCTUARY OF LA VERNA

SANCTUARY OF LA VERNA Mount La Verna was offered as a gift to St Francis in 1213, by Count Orlando Cattanei. This is the place where the Saint ultimately sealed with the stigmata in September 1224. Besides offering beautiful landscapes, the place is a very suggestive religious centre, where St Francis' presence is still pretty much tangible, as in the GROTTO, where he went to pray (with his stone bed still there for all to see), or in his CELL, where he retired in strict penitence, or even at the SASSO SPICCO, a rock suspended in the void for centuries. Also worth visiting is the CHURCH OF SANTA MARIA DEGLI ANGELI, built by St Francis between 1216 and 1218, later reworked and internally decorated with terracottas by Andrea della Robbia, among which stands the magnificent enamelled-terracotta altar-frontal with *Our Lady's Assumption*.

Sanctuary of La Verna

SANCTUARY MUSEUM Set up in a XV-century environment, the museum displays vestments, crucifixes, frescoes, choir books and other objects (XV-XVI century); this is where the "foco commune", a room in the middle of which a fire would burn non-stop during the winter, was reproduced.

Sanctuary of La Verna, wooden Cross

CHIESA MAGGIORE or BASILICA Started in 1348 and completed in 1509, it has a single-nave interior, housing some relics of St Francis and decorated with some superb glazed terracottas by Andrea della Robbia.

CHURCH OF THE STIGMATA Built in 1263, the Church features a single-nave interior, decorated with terracottas by Andrea and Luca della Robbia. A stone slab on its floor bears the inscription indicating the place where St Francis received the Stigmata.

MORE TO SEE OUTSIDE AREZZO

Located in the enchanting Casentino woodlands, in the Northern Apennines, the

Camaldoli, Monastery of the Carthusian Monks

MONASTERY OF THE CARTHUSIAN MONKS is situated along a winding road (in the midst of the protected forest, national park since 1991) leading to the Hermitage. Camaldoli monastery was built in 1046 on the ancient Castle of Fontebuona and was repeatedly reworked and enlarged over the following centuries. It nowadays counts 20 cells divided in five rows; they feature rectangular little houses overlooking a little porch and a vegetable garden. Besides the monastery, there is the CHURCH OF SANTI DONATO AND ILARIO and the guest-rooms, along with an ancient pharmacy, dated 1543, where the monks sell their homemade natural products. The HERMITAGE was the first seat of the Order that St Romualdo set up. He built five cells and an oratory here in 1012. Also worth visiting is the CHURCH OF OUR SAVIOUR, consecrated in 1027 and reshaped into a Baroque church after a fire that largely destroyed it; its single-nave interior houses several artworks.

Other interesting spots near Arezzo:

Caprese Michelangelo, Michelangelo Buonarroti's birthplace

CAPRESE MICHELANGELO This was the birthplace of the great Maestro Michelangelo Buonarroti, who was born here on March 6, 1475, a time when his father Lodovico, born in Florence, held a position as podestà in the town. News of this small town is available since little before the year 1000; the whereabouts of political events brought it under the rule of Florence in 1384. Michelangelo was therefore born in the PODESTÀ'S HOUSE, a small XIV-century building still open to the public and recently restored. It accommodates an interesting museum fully dedicated to Michelangelo, displaying pictures and casts of the famous works by this man of genius. Just outside the house there is a monument dedicated to Michelangelo, made by Armando Zocchi in 1911.

CASENTINO FOREST It is one of the most relevant natural beauties of Arezzo province, with its age-old woods, its many little towns and glorious castles. The river Arno originates in this region, from a spring at the slopes of Mount Falterona. The landscape, enclosed in a deep valley surrounded by hills and mountains, is of paramount beauty.

POPPI The town is situated on an isolated hill in the heart of the Casentino region. Documents provide evidence of Poppi being an important town already in 1169. It was the residence of the Counts Guidi, Florence's enemies, who, after the battle of Anghiari, were banned from their possessions and Poppi was definitely brought under the rule of the Florentine Republic as a start, to come under the rule of the Medici family afterwards. Mino da Fiesole (approximately 1430-84) and

Poppi,
Castle of the Counts Guidi

Poppi himself (Francesco Morandini 1544-97) were born here. The town is dominated by the CASTLE OF THE COUNTS GUIDI, and by the Praetorian Palace, started at the end of the XII century, rebuilt in 1274 and enlarged in 1291, perhaps to the design of Arnolfo di Cambio, to be finally restored in this century of ours. Its facade is divided into two parts by the tall tower; the right portion is the most ancient. All the castle is decorated with square-topped battlements. Its suggestive rooms are decorated with plenty of artworks. A must-see is also the Church of San Fedele, built between 1185 and 1195 and restored between 1928 and 1934. Its Latin-cross, single-nave interior displays several paintings dating back to the XVI and to the XVII centuries.

Stia

STIA Situated at the slopes of Mount Falterona, it is a wealthy town, due to the significant development of the textile industry, situated right where the Staggia creek meets with the river Arno. The town developed in the Middle Ages and still hosts a quarter with the PARISH CHURCH OF SANTA MARIA ASSUNTA, repeatedly reworked over the centuries and featuring an XVIII-century facade. The PALAGIO CASTLE was raised on the ancient residence of the Counts Guidi; destroyed in 1440, it was built again in a medieval style by Giuseppe Castellucci in 1908.

PIAN DI SCÓ This is a small agricultural town situated in the midst of vineyards and olive groves. Its parish church, dedicated to the Virgin Mary, dates back to the XII-XIII century.
Its three-nave interior houses beautiful capitals carved with figures and a fresco dating back to the XV century, found during the restoration works in 1934.

Stia, bell tower

PIEVE SANTO STEFANO This ancient town underwent several dominations throughout the Middle Ages, until, in 1387, it came under the rule of Florence. In 1855, it was almost entirely destroyed by a flood, whereas, in 1944, it was almost razed to the ground by the withdrawing German troops. The heart of this town hosts the Collegiate Church of Santo Stefano, rebuilt in 1844 on the ruins of a XIII century church. The fresco on its facade, featuring St Stephen, dates back to 1930. Its Latin-cross, three-nave interior houses some beautiful glazed terracottas dating back to the XV and the XVI centuries. Among these is the *Assumption and Saints*, presumably by Andrea della Robbia (1514).

Stia, Castle of Porciano

M. Fumaiolo
▲ 1407

Passo
dei Mandrioli

oppi

Bibbiena

San Sepolcro ○

larno

AREZZO ◇

Castiglion
Fiorentino ○

○
Cortona

Lago
ontepulciano

ulciano

M. Cetona
1148 ▲

dia S. Salvatore

dente ○

GROSSETO
- DUOMO OF SAN LORENZO
- DIOCESAN MUSEUM OF SACRED ART
- ARCHAEOLOGICAL MUSEUM
- CHURCH OF SAN FRANCESCO
- THE CITY WALLS

ITS SURROUNDINGS:
- ISLE OF GIGLIO
- MASSA MARITTIMA
- MOUNT AMIATA
- PITIGLIANO
- PORTO ERCOLE
- ROSELLE
- SOVANA
- MAREMMA
- ISLE OF GIANNUTRI
- CAPALBIO
- ORBETELLO
- MOUNT ARGENTARIO
- PORTO SANTO STEFANO
- PARCO DELL'UCCELLINA
- MAGLIANO IN TOSCANA
- SATURNIA TERME
- SORANO

GROSSETO AND ITS SURROUNDINGS

GROSSETO

Grosseto is the main town in Maremma, situated in the heart of a marshland that was only drained on a permanent basis in the XIX century, under the rule of the House of Lorraine. The area was already hosting human settlements during the Etruscan and Roman period, as shown by archaeological finds. Other archaeological excavations with ruins of the ancient settlement are in Roselle, in the neighbourhood of Grosseto. The town was founded by the Etruscans in the VII century B.C. Grosseto was initially a small fief of the Counts Aldobrandeschi, contended by the Sienese (XI century), who succeeded in conquering it only in 1336. When, in 1559, the town was taken over by the Medici family along with Siena, it experienced an outstanding economic growth (in 1574, Francesco I built the city walls and started to drain the swampy surroundings), but could not radically solve the problems caused by malaria. It was with Leopold II of the House of Lorraine (since 1828) that new impetus was given to the draining works, to be only completed in the XX century.

The territory of Grosseto is a very interesting area both for its natural landscapes and for its artistic tradition. The town municipal territory includes four different protected areas: the *wildlife reserve Diaccia Botrona, the nature reserve of Maremma* (the park is situated among the mouth of the river Ombrone, the coastline and the Uccellina Mountains) and the *Formiche di Grosseto*, little rocks to be found in both the *Arcipelago Toscano Natural Park* and in the *Santuario dei Cetacei* (cetacean sanctuary), an internationally protected sea area, which also includes the coastline of the Town of Grosseto and its waterfront.

Palazzo Aldobrandeschi,
in plain sight the Monument
known as *Canapone*

Grosseto,
Duomo of San Lorenzo

DUOMO OF SAN LORENZO (Piazza Dante) It was built in the years 1294-1302 by Sozzo di Rustichino, on the ruins of a pre-existing church, erected in 1190. Unfortunately, its facade has lost its original aspect, due to the interventions carried out from 1816 to 1855. Even its triple-nave interior no longer features the original decorations by Sozzo da Rustichino from Siena, due to the remakes carried out from the XVI to the XIX century. Noteworthy are a *Baptismal Font* and the *Altar dedicated to Our Lady of Grace*, both by Antonio di Palo Ghini, made between 1470 and 1474, as well as the superb *Virgin of Grace* by Matteo di Giovanni, also made in 1470.

ARCHAEOLOGICAL AND ART MUSEUM OF MAREMMA – DIOCESAN MUSEUM OF SACRED ART (Piazza Baccarini). These museums house interesting archaeological sections from prehistory to the Middle Ages, donated by Canon Chelli (who also founded the museum), and a collection of works that belonged to the Diocesan Sacred Art Collection. The archaeological Museum displays Etruscan archaeological relics from the excavations of Talamone, Roselle, Populonia and Vetulonia; the Museum of Sacred Art mostly contains works of the Sienese tradition, ranging from the XIII to the XVII century. Among the masterpieces housed here is the *Virgin of the Cherries* by Sassetta.

CHURCH OF SAN FRANCESCO (Piazza Indipendenza) Erected on a pre-existing Benedictine building, abandoned in 1220, it was bought by the Franciscan Friars, who rebuilt it around 1289. Its gothic facade is enriched by a portal and a rose window. Its one-nave interior houses many remarkable works of art, among which a *Crucifix* by Duccio da Boninsegna stands out.

THE CITY WALLS Unfolding on an octagonal plan to the design of Baldassarre Lanci, they were erected by Grand Duke Francesco I, in 1574, partially maintaining the medieval walls. In 1835, Leopold II transformed all battlements and bastions into promenades and gardens of public domain. Their North-East corner features the MEDICEAN FORTRESS, built in the XVI century for military purposes.

Isle of Giglio

ISLE OF GIGLIO

ISLE OF GIGLIO This is the second biggest island (after the Isle of Elba) of the Tuscan Archipelago for its surface area, entirely mountainous. It features a rocky coastline that is mainly to be reached by sea, perfect for an aquatic sport like underwater fishing. The island has been inhabited since prehistoric times and also became an important Etruscan port.

In the III century B.C. it was seized by the Romans and, in the Middle Ages, it passed into the hands of several families and also belonged to several cities. In 1554, the island was attacked by Pirate Khair Addin Barbarossa, who reduced most of its inhabitants to slavery. In 1558, it was merged into the Grand Duchy of Tuscany. The three towns to be found on the island are: Giglio Porto, Giglio Castello and Campese. Its climate is particularly mild, ideal for holidays at any time of the year.

MASSA MARITTIMA The town is situated in the heart of the mining area, on the Metalliferous Hills from which miners once extracted lead, silver and copper. It was probably an Etruscan town and also an important one, until, in 935, it was destroyed by the Saracens and only slowly recovered.

Isle of Giglio,
a glimpse on the port

After a series of political alliances, the town passed, in 1555, under the rule of the Medici family. Malaria caused mass casualties until, in the XIX century, the House of Lorraine carried out some major drainage works in the surrounding marshlands.

This area is rich in copper, wood coal, alum, iron, pyrite and other minerals. The first mineral reporting code of Europe was written here in 1310.

Massa Marittima, Duomo

DUOMO (Piazza Garibaldi) Started in the XIII century to form a Romanesque-Gothic building, its apsidal volume was enlarged between 1287 and 1304.

The lintel of its central portal features a remarkable Romanesque bas-relief, depicting *Scenes from the life of San Cerbone* (to whom the Cathedral is dedicated). Its quadrangular bell tower dates back to the XIII century, although it was largely reconstructed after 1920.

In its triple-nave interior lies a FONT carved from a single block of travertine by Giroldo da Como, in 1267. Besides this, the Cathedral houses other works of art dated XIII to XVII century.

Massa Marittima,
Town Hall

THE TOWN HALL (Piazza Garibaldi) This Romanesque building is made up of two jointed tower-houses of the XIII and the XIV century respectively, by Sienese architects.

PRAETORIAN PALACE (Piazza Garibaldi) Previously the Palace of the Podestà, it was built in travertine in the XIII century. Its facade features the coat of arms of the Podestàs that held power from 1426 to 1633. It accommodates the Archaeological Museum and the Art Gallery.

Also worth visiting: the MINING MUSEUM (Via Corridoni), situated into an exhausted mine, the ARCO DEI SENESI (Piazza Matteotti), the CHURCH OF SAN AGOSTINO (Corso Armando Diaz), built in a Romanesque-Gothic style, and the FORTEZZA DEI SENESI, built after 1335 and destroyed four centuries later to build the Hospital of Sant'Andrea.

Mount Amiata,
Skiing facilities

MOUNT AMIATA Amiata is the modern name of the ancient *Mons Tuniae*, also known as *Mons ad Meata* (m. 1738), situated among the Maremma, the Orcia Valley and the Chiana Valley. Mount Amiata is an ancient, cone-shaped volcano, extinct for centuries. By virtue of the extraordinary porosity of its rocks, it is scattered with several water springs at an altitude of 500 to 1,000 m. Besides the water springs, Mount Amiata has several mines, some of which are still in use, producing mercuric-sulphide (cinnabar) that, once processed, takes on a range of colours from orange-red to violet-red.

On Mount Amiata, easily reached through a tangle of roads, there are ski slopes equipped with ski lift systems, turning the Mountain into a famous winter tourist resort. All around Mount Amiata are the ancient towns of ABBADIA SAN SALVATORE, PIANCASTAGNAIO, ARCIDOSSO, CASTEL DEL PIANO, SANTA FIORA, CASTELL'AZZARA, to list just a few, that offer magnificent panoramic views and are worth visiting.

PITIGLIANO Erected on a tufa plateau that drops sheer to the river Lente, the town features houses built at the top of sheer tufa cliffs, almost rising from them. It was initially an Etruscan town passed to the Romans, then to the Aldobrandeschi family during the Middle Ages, to end up under the rule of the Orsini family. In 1608, it joined the Grand Duchy of Tuscany.

Already in the XV century Pitigliano was the home of a thriving Jewish community which dwindled in numbers after the last war. Evidence of its presence is provided by the Synagogue and the

Pitigliano

Jewish Quarters. Worth visiting is PALAZZO ORSINI, in the town centre, a XIV-century Palace, enlarged in the XV century by Niccolò II Orsini, and, in the XVI century, by Niccolò IV, to the design of Giuliano da Sangallo. The DUOMO, dedicated to Santi Pietro and Paolo, is situated in Piazza Gregorio VII. The Medieval, one-nave Cathedral underwent vast modifications in the XVI-XIX centuries, still visible in the interior and on its facade. Its mighty bell tower houses a 3-tonne bell.

Last but not least, the ETRUSCAN MUSEUM displays several archaeological relics found in the surroundings.

PORTO ERCOLE The town is a famous seaside resort situated in a bay, on the Argentario Eastern coast. The modern town is equipped to welcome tourists, whereas the ancient town still preserves and conveys the evocative charm of an ancient fishermen's village. Previously called *Portus Herculis* by the Romans, the town still displays an ancient entrance gate, leading to the inhabited area characterised by steep staircases. Piazza Santa Barnaba is dominated by the PALAZZO CONSANI (XVI century), that was the Spanish Governor's palace; whereas, the upper town is dominated by the ROCCA, a defensive structure hosting the fortresses of SANTA BARBARA, MONTE FILIPPO and STELLA, built to the design of Giovan Battista Bellucci (1506-54). The town parish church houses the tomb of Caravaggio, who died on July 8, 1610, on the nearby beach of Cala Galera.

ROSELLE This is an ancient Etruscan town, probably under the Roman rule in 294 B.C., for Plinio refers to it as a Roman colony. Over the centuries, it suffered Barbarian and Saracens incursions, which led to the town's premature decline. The Etruscan walls of the ancient settlement are left almost intact, with their perimeter extending for about 3,200 metres and its six gates. Built with huge blocks of stone, they were reinforced in the late Roman period, when the whole town was enlarged with monuments that are still visible, such as the small amphitheatre, the forum and a road along which an Augustan Basilica and a basilica dedicated to the imperial cult, dating back to the Julio-Claudian era, are to be found. The Northern part of the town still hosts some particularly relevant Etruscan buildings; these were dwellings built in raw brick and stone masonry, cemented with clay and plastered, dating back to the VII and V century B.C. These ruins are very rare, for the material used to build them is highly perishable. Last but not least, Roselle also hosts the so-called Villa, which was probably a thermal facility back in the I century A.D. Outside the walls lie the ruins of a small necropolis, also featuring some chamber tombs.

Roselle, Archaeological Park

Roselle, Archaeological Park, detail of a mosaic

SOVANA This is an ancient Etruscan town and even one of the most important back in the VII and VI centuries B.C. It fell under the rule of the Romans, the Lombards, the Aldobrandeschi and the Orsini families. Inexorably the town gradually declined and, despite its being built atop of a hill, its population was hit by malaria. Although the Government of the Grand Duchy provided the town with sewages, aqueducts and also refurbished the houses where some of the refugees from Lorraine were housed, their efforts to stop the exodus of its inhabitants were to no avail. Still visible are the ruins of the ROCCA ALDOBRANDESCA, a XIII-century fortress, restored in 1572 and destroyed in the XVII century, and the Romanesque small CHURCH OF SANTA MARIA (XII century), featuring a triple-nave interior, housing a travertine *Cyborium* of the VIII-IX century. The DUOMO, dedicated to Santi Pietro and Paolo, is a Romanesque building, though different styles have been overlapping over the centuries. Upon leaving Sovana, you will reach the ETRUSCAN NECROPOLIS, almost entirely made of chamber-tombs, carved in the walls of Fosso Calesina. The main perimeter of the site dates back to the IV-III century B.C. and it stands out as an important archaeological site, due to the range of its architectural decorations, carved in tufa and still visible.

Sovana

Sovana, Ildebranda Tomb

MORE TO SEE OUTSIDE GROSSETO

Castiglion della Pescaia

MAREMMA Such is called the Southern coastal area in Tuscany, stretching from the river Cecina (in the province of Livorno), to Tarquinia (in the province of Viterbo). Originally inhabited by the Etruscans, with their powerful cities, it suffered a rapid decline after the fall of the Roman Empire, besides being hit by malaria. It was only with Leopold II of Tuscany that, in 1828, the drainage works, that were only to be completed in the XX century, commenced. Today Maremma is a region with fairly developed livestock, agricultural and mining sectors. Most of its income comes from the tourist industry, pretty well established in the towns of CASTIGLIONE DELLA PESCAIA, MARINA DI GROSSETO, MARINA DI CECINA, FOLLONICA, PORTO SANTO STEFANO and ORBETELLO.

Giannutri, Cala Maestra

ISLE OF GIANNUTRI This is the most Southerly island of the Tuscan Archipelago. It features a largely rocky coast, with only two gravel beaches, known as CALA DELLO SPALMATOIO and CALA MAESTRA respectively, the only landing places of the island. During the Roman Empire a port and a villa were built here, the ruins of which are still visible. It later remained uninhabited for centuries and occasionally provided a shelter to the Corsairs. When, in 1861, it joined the Kingdom of Italy, the LIGHTHOUSE OF CAPEL ROSSO was built on the far end tip of the island bearing the same name.

CAPALBIO This is a renowned tourist resort in the South of Tuscany, offering beautiful beaches and shady woods. In September, it holds the traditional festival of the *wild boar* (*sagra del cinghiale*), an animal living in the surrounding area covered with the Mediterranean Scrub. Capalbio underwent several dominations during the Middle Ages. It is still surrounded by its ancient, XV-century walls, featuring the beautiful SIENESE GATE. The town still hosts the PARISH CHURCH OF SAN NICOLA, with its Romanesque capitals, dating back to the XII century, and works of art of the XV and the XVI centuries.

Capalbio

ORBETELLO Erected on a stretch of land in the middle of the lagoon, it is situated within the ruins of the Etruscan walls and of the better preserved Sienese and Spanish fortified structures (XVI century).
From 1557 to 1815 it was the capital of the small Spanish state of Presidi (including Porto Ercole, Talamone, Porto Santo Stefano and Mount Argentario), and later passed under the rule of the Grand Duchy of Tuscany. A three-arch gate of the Spanish fortifications (1557-1620), known as PORTA DEL SOCCORSO, provides entrance to the town hosting the DUOMO dedicated to Santa Maria Assunta. Erected in 1376, it was rebuilt in the XVII century.

The sea at Orbetello

MOUNT ARGENTARIO Very renowned and popular as a nautical holiday and seaside resort, Mount Argentario is an elliptical promontory, connected to the coast by two sand bars, delimiting the Orbetello lagoon; Argentario was originally an island, only connected to the mainland by the sand bars that were created after the waters began to stilt up.

PORTO SANTO STEFANO Seat of the Local government of Mount Argentario, Porto Santo Stefano is also a famous seaside resort, besides being an important fishing town since the XV century, when it was erected by fishermen from Liguria and from the Isle of Elba.
The ancient inhabited centre was almost entirely destroyed during World War II, following fearsome air and naval bombings. Ferries leave from its port, made up of a PORTO VECCHIO and a PORTO NUOVO, for the Isle of Giglio.

Mount Argentario
Porto Santo Stefano

Natural Park of Uccellina,
bay of Cala Forno

Natural Park of Uccellina,
Palaeolithic grottoes

PARCO DELL'UCCELLINA The area of the Uccellina Mountains has been a Natural Park since 1975, so as to prevent any alteration of its uncontaminated nature. It is entirely covered with a thick forest vegetation (Mediterranean Scrub), amidst of which rise the ancient towers and religious buildings, providing evidence of the past human presence in this territory. Among these, worth visiting are the ABBEY OF SAN RABANO, a largely tumbledown building, the TOWERS OF CASTELMARINO, COLLE-LUNGO, CALA DI FORNO and BELLA MARSILIA.

MAGLIANO IN TOSCANA Situated on the crest of a hill, the town still maintains its medieval appearance, even though the first settlement dates back to the Etruscans. Its walls, still fairly well preserved, were designed by a Sienese architect of the first half of the XV century, who partially used the pre-existing XIII-century wall ring, built for the Aldobrandeschi family. PORTA NUOVA is the gateway leading to the inhabited centre, where a must-see is the Romanesque CHURCH OF SAN MARTINO, built before the year 1000 and first restored to meet the Gothic taste. More recent restoration works were carried out after the last war. Also worth seeing is the PALAZZO DEI PRIORI, built in 1430, and the CHURCH OF SAN GIOVANNI BATTISTA, a Romanesque building, featuring, though, a beautiful Renaissance facade (1471).

SATURNIA TERME The pre-Etruscan town was also under the dominion of the Romans. In the XIV century, Saturnia Terme was destroyed by the Sienese, for it had become a base for the outcasts. People come here for its renowned thermal baths, where a spring of sulphuric water (37.5°C.) is used to treat a number of diseases. Everybody can freely enjoy a bath in the sulphurous waters of the Gorello waterfalls, on the road to Montemerano.

Saturnia, thermal baths

SORANO Erected on a tufa spur overlooking the Lente Valley, the town is still surrounded by its medieval fortified walls. Originally an Etruscan town, it was under the dominion of the Aldobrandeschi and the Orsini families, until it passed under the rule of the Grand Duchy of Tuscany in 1608. It rises within the archaeological area known as PARCO ARCHEOLOGICO DEL TUFO, including several Etruscan necropolises, interconnected by a coeval maze of streets, unfolding among the steep walls of tufa. Particularly interesting are the Etruscan tombs found near the town. Absolutely worth visiting is the ROCCA DEGLI ORSINI, a beautiful example of Renaissance military architecture. Two imposing corner bastions are connected by a wall, in the middle of which is the main gate. Its interior still shows remains of the premises intended for the ladies and the garrison of the Rocca. The MIDDLE AGES AND RENAISSANCE MUSEUM has its seat here. It houses glazed ceramics, manuscripts and frescoes.

Following some recent conservative restoration works, an interesting cycle of frescoes by the Sienese school has been brought to surface. The COLLEGIATE CHURCH OF SAN NICOLA has been entirely restored in the XVIII century. Its interior houses the relics of San Felicissima, brought to Sorano from the Roman catacombs, in 1772. Also noteworthy is a wooden *Crucifix*, donated by Grand Duke Cosimo III de'Medici (1642-1723), a painting depicting *St Dominic*, attributed to the school of Francesco Vanni (1587-1657) and another depicting *St Joseph and Child* by Pietro Aldi (1884).

Sorano, Orsini Palace

Sorano

LONIGIANA

Passo
della Cisa

M. Sillara
1861

Pontremoli

Alpe di Succiso
2017
Passo del
Cerreto

Fivizzano
1894

Aulla

M. La Nuda

GARFAGNANA

Sarzana

M. Pisanino
1945

Alpi Apuane

VERSILIA

Pania della Croce
1858

CARRARA

MASSA

Forte dei Marmi

Camaiore

Viareggio

Lago di
Massaciuccoli

M. Giovo
1991

Passo
dell'Abetone

Barga

S. Marcello
Pistoiese

M. Calvi
1283

Firenzuola   1031

M. Fago

Passo della
Raticosa

Passo
della Futa

MUGELLO

Alpe S. Be

Le Pizzorne
1026

Montecatini
Terme

PISTOIA

Borgo
S. Lorenzo

M. Giovi   992

Monti di Calvana

Bagni di Lucca

LUCCA

Pescia

Capannori

Monsummano
Terme M. Albano
627

PRATO

Signa

Sesto Fiorentino

FIRENZE

Pontass

S. Giuliano
Terme

917
M. Pisano

PISA

Cascina

Pontedera

San Casciano
in Val di Pesa

Impruneta

Reg

Montespertoli

Figline Valdarno

Greve
892

Marina di Pisa

Tirrenia

Certaldo

M. S. Michele

CHIANTI

LIVORNO ◉

Castiglioncello

onsi

SIENA

Isola di Gorgona
(Livorno)

Rosignano Solvay

Montagnola
663

Cecin

e

Le Crete

TIRRENO

S. Vin

re

Capraia

Montalcino

Isola di Capraia
(Livorno)

Golfo di Bara

Populon

da

ARCIPELAGO

Canale di Pio

Piom

Arcidosso

M. Labb
1193

Portoferraio

Marciana

Isola d'Elba
(Livorno)

M. Capanne
1018

Por

SSETO

M. Faete
770

Marina di Campo

Punta dei

Saturnia

Punta del Marchese

Piti

Pianosa

Isola di Pianosa
(Livorno)

Tala

516
M. Bellir

TOSCA

Scoglio d'Africa

Isola di
Montecristo
(Livorno)

glio
eto)

annutri
sseto)

itinerary

LIVORNO
- PIAZZA GRANDE
- THE TOWN HALL
- MEDICEAN DISTRICT
- BATTINI DELL'OLIO
- CHURCH OF SAN FERDINANDO
- FORTEZZA VECCHIA
- PIAZZA GIUSEPPE MICHELI
- MEDICEAN PORT
- CHURCH OF THE CONCEZIONE
- CISTERNINO
- FORTEZZA NUOVA
- FOSSO REALE
- PALAZZO DE LARDEREL
- CISTERNONE
- CHURCH OF MADONNA DEL SOCCORSO
- VILLA FABBRICOTTI

ITS SURROUNDINGS:
- CAPRAIA
- ISLE OF ELBA
- PORTOFERRAIO
- MARCIANA ALTA
- MARCIANA MARINA
- MARINA DI CAMPO
- CAPOLIVERI
- PORTO AZZURRO
- RIO MARINA
- POPULONIA
- SANCTUARY OF MONTENERO

LIVORNO
AND ITS SURROUNDINGS

LIVORNO, THE MEDICEAN TOWN

Mention of a town called *Livorna* is made in some ancient documents dating back to 1017. It served as a port for the Pisans and presumably had its own castle in the year 1000. It was later turned into the fortified Port of Pisa (1392), into that of the Viscontis from Milan, before it became the port of Genoa (1405), selling it to Florence in 1421. Livorno was then ruled by the Medici Family and turned into the most important sea Port of the whole State of Tuscany, and eventually consolidated its role under the Grand Dukedom, due to the policies of Cosimo I and Cosimo II. The new Port was started in 1571 and the town was granted a new organisation in 1576. However, it was with the 1593 "Constitution" that Livorno became a unique example of its kind, when immigrants of all races and religions were granted full freedom to reside there. Furthermore, when the Medicean Port was finished, in 1618, Livorno was declared a free port, and became economically powerful to the extent that it rose to eminence as the second most important town of Tuscany by the end of the XVIII century.

When annexed to the Kingdom of Italy, Livorno grew even further, due to its commercial activities, also supported by industrial activities and tourism. Despite the heavy damage suffered during World War II, it is still the core of all economic activities in the region: even today its Port is the most important in Tuscany, and one of the most important in the Mediterranean. It is divided into Porto Vecchio situated in the Southern part of the town (the Medicean Port) with its Dockyards (the old and the new one) and Basins of Mandraccio, and the Porto Nuovo at the North, connected to the aforementioned by the Canale delle Industrie. Livorno was hometown to famous people such as: Francesco Domenico Guerrazzi (1804-73), Giovanni Fattori (1825-1908), Plinio Nomellini (1866-1943), Amedeo Modigliani (1884-1920), Pietro Mascagni (1863-1945). The pentagonal structure of the city centre was modelled on the XVI-century theories of the ideal city; it is evidence of its past splendour, indelibly destroyed by the air raids during World War II, as well as by the choices its administrators made with regard to the strategies for its reconstruction.

Medicean Fortress
or *Fortezza Vecchia*

Duomo

Town Hall

Medicean District

Fortezza Vecchia

Piazza Giuseppe Micheli,
Monument of Ferdinand I
also known as the *Four Moors*

THE OLD TOWN

PIAZZA GRANDE This is the heart of the old town of Livorno; it was rebuilt after the 1943 bombings. At the south stands the DUOMO dedicated to San Francesco from Assisi. Built between 1594 and 1606, it was enlarged in the XVIII century and largely rebuilt to its original XVI-century design by Alessandro Pieroni after World War II. It is designed in the shape of a Latin cross with one nave, which gives it a very simple and sober appearance.

THE TOWN HALL It was built in 1720 to the design of Giovanni del Fantasia. Heavily damaged during the earthquake in 1742, it was largely rebuilt in 1745. Bombed during World War II, a whole section of it was destroyed. However, what remains of its original and most ancient section still features examples of fine workmanship.

MEDICEAN DISTRICT also known as VENEZIA NUOVA This district formed after the curtain between the Old and the New Fortress had been demolished (1629-44); its dwellings soon became a home to dockers and fishermen and still are.

BATTINI DELL'OLIO (Viale Caprera) These oil stores are worth a visit. Built in 1705 for Cosimo III, they were enlarged in 1731 for Gian Gastone, to the design of G.B. Foggini. This large complex includes 304 oil-tight masonry containers lined with slate, with an overall capacity of approximately 24,000 barrels of oil.

CHURCH OF SAN FERDINANDO or CHURCH OF THE CROCETTA It was built between 1707-14. The structure by Giovan Battista Foggini was largely damaged during the war and only recently restored. Its single-nave structure features an interior decorated with statues, stuccos and marbles that make it renowned as one of the most beautiful churches in Livorno.

FORTEZZA VECCHIA Built by Antonio da Sangallo the Young for Cardinal Gulio de'Medici (later to become Clement VII), the Old Fortress includes various superimposed fortified structures (1521-34) like the MASTIO DI MATILDE (IX century) and the QUADRATURA DEI PISANI (1377). The large, fortified structure, with its perimeter stretching for half a km, has two gates: Duke Alessandro de' Medici's gate, adorned by both the family coat of arms and the inscription *Sotto una fede et legge un signor solo* (*one faith, one law, one lord*), and the gate Maria de' Medici walked through when she left for France to marry the King (Henry IV). Furthermore, what is known as the Vecchia Darsena witnessed the departure of Amerigo Vespucci and Gianni da Verrazzano for the "New World".

PIAZZA GIUSEPPE MICHELI This square hosts the famous *Monument to Ferdinand I*, also referred to as the *Four Moors* by people in Livorno. The statue features Grand Duke Ferdinand I in his uniform as Grand Master of the Knights of St Stephen. It was originally erected by G. Bandini in 1595; the four statues by P. Tacca, featuring chained Barbary slaves (the Moors) were added in 1626.

MEDICEAN PORT It hosts the *Fortino della Sassaia* and the pier known as *Molo Cosimo (named after Cosimo II, who completed it in 1620),* as well as a number of breakwaters, among which is the *Dam of Marzocco*, named after the ancient octagonal *Tower of Marzocco*, erected by the Florentines in 1439 and decorated with a wind rose and the four coat of arms of the Republic of Florence.

CHURCH OF THE CONCEZIONE or CHURCH OF THE MADONNA Built to the design of Alessandro Pieroni in 1599, the church of the Holy Conception became a reference point for the many communities of foreigners settled in Livorno, who equipped it with their National altars. Its interior, shaped in a rectangular form, is made of a single nave featuring the altars of the foreign nations along its sides.

Medicean Port

CISTERNINO Built to the design of Pasquale Poccianti in 1842, this elegant water tank, meant to supply the town with drinking water, is almost unique in its neoclassic shape. Today it accommodates the *Casa della Cultura*.

FORTEZZA NUOVA Erected in 1590 by Vincenzo Bonanni and Bernardo Buontalenti, to the design of Giovanni de Medici, the New Fortress was originally joined to the old one by a wall. It was partially demolished to make room to the Venezia Nuova and the San Marco districts (1629-44).

FOSSO REALE The canal bounding the old town was erected to defend the bastions of the Medicean district; it overlooks the characteristic old districts.

Fortezza Nuova

THE MODERN CITY

PALAZZO DE LARDEREL (Via De Larderel) Built for Francesco de Larderel, who pioneered into the Tuscan boracid industry, the neoclassic palace was erected between 1832 and 1850. It nowadays accommodates the Civil Court.

CISTERNONE (Piazza del Cisternone) This Neoclassical structure designed by Pasquale Poccianti was erected between 1829 and 1832 to store the water of the Cològnole springs.

CHURCH OF THE MADONNA DEL SOCCORSO (Piazza della Vittoria) It is the biggest Church in Livorno. It was built during the first half of the XIX century, when, after the violent outbreak of cholera, a group of citizens raised funds to ask the Virgin Mary for protection. Built to the design of Gaetano Gherardi, the church was started in 1836 to be completed in 1856. Its interior, in the form of a Latin cross, is divided into three naves. Its structure echoes Brunelleschi's Renaissance architecture, though it incorporates internal pillars, simple and light in their design, that are evocative of a neoclassical style.

Palazzo de Larderel, interior, Ballroom

VILLA FABBRICOTTI Situated in the heart of a beautiful public garden, the elegant XIX-century building now accommodates the BIBLIOTECA LABRONICA (the town library) and GIOVANNI FATTORI CIVIC MUSEUM, which houses a nice collection of works by Fattori and by other Tuscan artists, among which are Michele Gordigiani, Amedeo Modigliani, Oscar Ghiglia, Plinio Nomellini, Vincenzo Cabianca, Giovanni Bartolena, Silvestro Lega to name just a few.

Naval Academy

The NAVAL ACADEMY is a source of pride for the town. Founded in 1881 by General Benedetto Brin of naval engineers, who merged Naples navy and Genoa Sardinian navy's schools, it was built in 1878 on the area of St Jacob and St Leopold's leper hospitals. The PANCALDI ACQUAVIVA BATHS are still to be seen along Livorno's seafront. Opened in 1846, they provide historic evidence of Livorno being a seaside resort.   .

THE SURROUNDINGS OF LIVORNO

Capraia

CAPRAIA It is a small island of the Tuscan Archipelago, with superb bays to be only reached by sea. A road stretches from its characteristic port to the small town of Capraia, dominated by the FORTRESS OF SAN GIORGIO, erected in the XV century by the Genoese, in order to defend themselves from the attacks by the Barbary pirates. The island also houses an agricultural penal colony. It is one of the few unspoilt places, still to be discovered by coastal tourist routes.

Isle of Elba, coastline

ISLE OF ELBA This is the largest island of the whole Tuscan Archipelago. Renowned for its mineral fields to the Etruscans (probably also to those who preceded them), who used to transport iron to Populonia, it was conquered by the Romans, the Genoese, the Lombards and by the Pisans. The Medici family as well as the Turkish had an interest in it and turned it into the target of their many incursions, along with the Spanish and the French, who, under their dominion, administratively annexed it to Tuscany (1809). From May 1814 to February 1815, Napoleon Bonaparte ruled over the island and its inhabitants, after choosing it as his home-in-exile. In 1815, the island was annexed to the Grand Duchy of Tuscany and, as part of it, to the Kingdom of Italy in 1860. Elba is nowadays one of the favourite tourist destinations for those who love nature and the seaside, for its magnificent stretch of coast, with its ideal sandy beaches, its cliffs and its rocky coastline. Its landscape features a succession of hills and mountains and is dominated by Mount Capanne (m. 1019).

Isle of Elba, Portoferraio

PORTOFERRAIO This is the main town on the island, where ferries from Piombino arrive. It is dominated by both *Forte Stella* and *Forte Falcone*, two fortresses built in 1548 by Cosimo I de' Medici. Situated in the upper part of the town, *Villa dei Mulini*, Napoleon's house (one of the three houses he held on the island of Elba), still features its original furniture and Napoleonic heirlooms. Not too far from Portoferraio there is *Napoleon's Villa of San Martino*, the exiled emperor's countryside residence; its interiors are decorated with some Egyptian-style frescoes, depicting the Egyptian campaigns of 1798 and 1799.

Portoferraio,
Napoleon's villa of S. Martino

MARCIANA ALTA The town was erected on the slopes of Mount Capanne (equipped with a cableway to reach the mountain top) and is dominated by the ruins of a castle built in 1015 by the Pisans; a must visit is the Civic Archaeological Museum, where remarkable archaeological finds from Elba are preserved.

MARCIANA MARINA

This is a famous seaside town, dominated by a round sighting tower, known as the SARACENS' TOWER, built in the XII century by the Pisans.

MARINA DI CAMPO This modern bathing resort is dominated by the TORRE DELLA MARINA, a tower dating back to the Medicean period.

CAPOLIVERI

This is a small town of miners situated on a hillock, offering a beautiful panoramic view.

PORTO AZZURRO Popular bathing resort, it was once just a small fishing town known as Porto Longone. Named after the fortress – today's jail – it was erected by Philip III of Spain, who, in 1603, built it as a defence against Pirates' incursions.

RIO MARINA

It is one of the most ancient towns on the island, due to the nearby iron mines (with reddish rocks still to be seen). Its town hall accommodates a small mining museum.

Elba, coastal inlet
of Punta Bianca

Populonia

POPULONIA Already an inhabited town during the iron age (IX century B.C.), it experienced a remarkable period of growth and development, due to its dominant position on a promontory. It was between the VII and the VI century B.C. that, known as Pupluna, the town witnessed a sharp increase in ore-mining (copper and iron) under the Etruscan, who also opened a sea Port in Porto Baratti. From the III century B.C., Populonia was under the Roman rule, with Romans taking all the iron production for themselves, which forced a slow and inevitable decline, also due to the siege by Silla, in 79 B.C., and to the pillages by Totila (546 A.D.) and the Lombards (570 A.D.). By the year 1000, what had long been a bloomtown had finally become uninhabited. Todays town dates back to the XIV century, when, after an attack by the Barbary Pirates, it was eventually surrounded by protective walls. A must visit is the ETRUSCAN MUSEUM displaying objects found in the tombs of the necropolis.

Town walls

THE ETRUSCAN NECROPOLIS Discovered and explored between 1908 and 1914, the necropolis overlooks the gulf of Baratti, close to what once was the Etruscan Port, later to become a Roman one. This site was used for burials from the IX to the III century B.C. Tombs were covered in the iron slag from the melting process, alternating with layers of coal, reddish rocks and cooked clay from the destroyed ovens; all these wastes have partially contributed to the conservation of the site; though the tomb roofs have been destroyed, the rooms and their furnishings are still pretty much well-preserved. On POGGIO DELLA PORCARECCIA, not so far from San Cerbone's Chapel, there is the *Flabelli Tomb*, named after the bronze fans, which, along with other gold, bucchero (black clay) and clay objects, made up the grave goods of the four deceased buried here. The tomb still has an intact pseudo-dome that covers it, dating back to the VII century B.C. Inside the burial chamber you can still see the stone beds that hosted the bodies. In the PODERE DI SAN CERBONE there are other visible tombs: the *Carts Tomb* (VII century B.C.) named after the cart found in one of its rooms; the T*omb of the funerary beds* and the *Tomb with vestibule*, featuring a small hall providing entrance to it. Close to them is the *Shrine Tomb* (V century B.C.), reproducing a cult shrine covered with a gable roof.

The shrine tomb known as the *Tomb of the Bronzetto Offerente*, is situated in the CASONE NECROPOLIS. It was named after a small

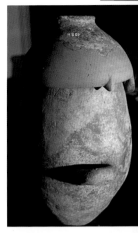

Etruscan Urn dating back to the IX century B.C.

Tomb of the Bronzetto Offerente

bronze statue originally attached to the cyma of a candelabrum and actually featuring an athlete throwing a discus. This is one of the most complete monuments, along with being among the best preserved ones. It dates back to the second half of the VI century B.C., so as to echo the power of the *polis*.

More single-room tombs, carved out of the tufa, are situated in the site known as LE GROTTE (II-I century B.C.), whereas small tombs in the form of chambers of the transitional period, from the Villanovian to the Etruscan period (VIII-VII century B.C.), have been arranged on POGGIO DELLE GRANATE.

Sanctuary of Montenero

SANCTUARY OF MONTENERO Following the route on leaving the city of Livorno, past Ardenza and Antignano, you will reach a sanctuary consecrated in 1575 and dedicated to the *Madonna delle Grazie* of Montenero.

Legend has it that in 1345 a limping shepherd found the image of the Virgin Mary asking him to take her on top of the Montenero hill; the shepherd agreed and was healed as a result.

OTHER INTERESTING PLACES

Bolgheri, Viale dei cipressi

next page:
Boccale Castle,
coastline of Livorno

Campiglia

Situated in the Southern Maremma, BOLGHERI, known for its famous *Viale dei Cipressi* (praised in the poem by Giosuè Carducci "Davanti San Guido"), is situated on a small hill, known for being the place where Giosuè Carducci spent his earliest youth, living in a house overlooking the town square, from 1832 to 1848. A few kilometres away, CASTAGNETO CARDUCCI was home to the famous poet from 1848 to 1849.

Both Bolgheri and Castagneto belonged to the Counts Della Gherardesca, who held a few castles in the area. Also worth visiting is CAMPIGLIA, an ancient town where the ruins of the medieval town walls are still visible, along with those of the Rocca (fortress), built in the VIII-IX century and restored between 1200 and 1300. It was the castle of the Della Gherardesca family. The Praetorian Palace (XV-XVI century) and the Florentine Gate are also still visible. Just out of town, erected in the old cemetery, the Parish Church of San Giovanni features a beautiful facade with polychrome marbles, dating back to 1163. A beautiful portal stands out on the side, featuring a lintel decorated with a peculiar bas-relief.

The small town of VENTURINA, situated on the Via Aurelia, near Campiglia, hosts the Caldana Baths, with waters gushing out from cracks in the soil at a temperature of 36-43°, channelled into the town hotel offering a range of pleasant and relaxing thermal treatments.

© Copyright 2011
This book has been edited and published by
ATS Italia Editrice s.r.l.
via di Brava, 41/43 - 00163 Roma
tel. 0666415961 - fax 0666512461
www.atsitalia.it
e-mail: atsitalia@atsitalia.it
Largo M. Liverani, 12/3 - 50141 Firenze
tel. 0554220577 - fax 0554220649
e-mail: atsitalia.firenze@atsitalia.it
No part of this book may be reproduced

Editorial co-ordination *Frida Giannini*
Photo research *Angela Giommi*
Graphic design, layout and cover *Susanna Tedeschi*
Scanning and colour correction *Leandro Ricci*
Technical co-ordination *Flavio Zancla*
Translation *Chiara Luisi*
Printing *Primaprint S.r.l. - Viterbo*
Photographs *Photographic archive Ats Italia Editrice*
      Photographic archive Electa
      Patrizio Del Duca
      Nicolò Orsi Battaglini

*The images from the Electa photographic archives reproducing
cultural assets that belong to the Italian State have been published
with the permission of the Italian Ministero dei Beni e le Attività Culturali*

*The publisher may be notified concerning
any unidentified iconographic sources*

Questo volume è disponibile anche in lingua italiana
Ce volume est disponible aussi en français
Dieser Band ist auch in deutscher Sprache erhältlich
Esta obra también está publicada en español

ISBN 978-88-6524-400-5